DATE DUE

ALLEGHENY CAMPUS LIBRARY
COMMUNITY COLLEGE OF ALLEGHENY COUNTY
808 RIDGE AVENUE
PITTSBURGH, PA 15212

DEMCO

AMERICAN LABOR

*FROM CONSPIRACY
TO
COLLECTIVE BARGAINING*

ADVISORY EDITORS

Leon Stein   *Philip Taft*

WOMEN AND THE LABOR MOVEMENT

Alice Henry

ARNO & THE NEW YORK TIMES
NEW YORK   1971

Reprint Edition 1971 by Arno Press Inc.

Reprinted from a copy in
The U.S. Department of Labor Library
LC# 70-156416
ISBN 0-405-02924-1

American Labor: From Conspiracy to Collective Bargaining—Series II
ISBN for complete set: 0-405-02910-1
See last pages of this volume for titles.

Manufactured in the United States of America

The Workers' Bookshelf

WOMEN AND THE LABOR MOVEMENT

ALICE HENRY

WOMEN AND THE LABOR MOVEMENT

BY
ALICE HENRY

MEMBER OF THE AMERICAN FEDERATION OF TEACHERS
SECRETARY, EDUCATIONAL DEPARTMENT, NATIONAL WOMEN'S TRADE UNION LEAGUE

NEW YORK
GEORGE H. DORAN COMPANY

COPYRIGHT, 1923,
BY GEORGE H. DORAN COMPANY

WOMEN AND THE LABOR MOVEMENT. III
PRINTED IN THE UNITED STATES OF AMERICA

TO
MY BROTHER ALFRED
IN AUSTRALIA
FAR AWAY IN DISTANCE
VERY NEAR IN THOUGHT

PREFACE

If the inhabitants of Earth were all of one sex, it might be a much duller world. It would assuredly be a much simpler world to run, an easier world to understand. It would probably be a less changeful world.

Yet how far less interesting!

The editors of this series understand that the presence of women in modern industry does add to the complexity of industrial problems, problems which men and women have to solve and to solve together. They therefore desired to include in the series some statement of the activities of women in the labor movement of the United States.

When they invited me to write a brief account of a large subject, I gladly agreed, even although on the understanding that the time allowed for preparation was, in proportion, briefer still.

I am therefore the more indebted to those who made the completion of the undertaking possible, by generously giving information and assistance. I especially wish to thank the staff of the Women's Bureau and the officers of the National Women's Trade Union League for such cooperation.

Dr. John B. Andrews' "History of Women in Trade Unions," Vol. X of the Federal Report on Woman and Child Wage Earners, remains the standard work of reference on the early attempts of women to organize and bargain collectively, although other authorities on women in industry have been consulted and are listed as references.

PREFACE

All important organizations with women members, whether within or without the American Federation of Labor, have been communicated with, but not all of the officials addressed have responded.

The accounts of the newer organizations are taken chiefly from their own official literature and printed records of their experiences and activities. Efforts were made also to secure other points of view, but not always with success.

I desire to thank the editors of the *New Republic* for permission to quote the editorial upon the Women's Division in the Bureau of Labor Statistics. John Davidson's poem "To the Generation Knocking at the Door" is reprinted by permission of the English publisher, E. Grant Richards.

Among those who have thus kindly assisted me in revising different sections are Professor Robert H. Lowie, Miss S. P. Breckinridge, Mrs. Irene Osgood Andrews, Miss Mary Van Kleeck, Dr. Alice Hamilton, Dr. Leo Wolman, Miss Mary W. Dewson, Professor Paul H. Douglas, Mrs. Mary Kenney O'Sullivan, Miss Anne Withington, and the officers of almost all the international unions with women members, which have been dealt with here.

I record here my thanks to Miss Sarah C. Rippey, to Miss Gail Wilson, and to Miss Frances Bird and other friends for additional assistance.

A few pages have seen the light previously, in *Life and Labor* and elsewhere.

It would be impossible to cover so much fresh ground without falling into some error. May I ask it as a favor from readers that they will be so kind as to let me know when they come across any such evidence of familiar human fallibility?

ALICE HENRY.

June, 1923.

INTRODUCTION

At this moment it is important, as never before, that the question of the employment of women in the industries of this country should be dealt with in a sane and reasonable fashion, and to that end it is essential that the opinions of the women who do the work should be canvassed and listened to. There is no better way of learning these views than as these are expressed through those women who are organized into unions; because time and experience have enabled them to form and express convictions upon women's special difficulties, and also in a measure to handle those difficulties as they arise locally. Besides, they are the only women quite free to express opinions without paying for freedom of speech in the loss of a job.

When power machinery was introduced into the United States somewhat over a hundred years ago, women were drawn into the service of machine industry. They came into it haphazard, and with no anticipation on the part of employer, fellow-workmen or the community of what this was going to mean to women themselves, or to the men beside whom they worked. So that modern industry, while it has enormously increased production of everything that can be grown or manufactured, has brought with it a whole array of new problems and new dangers, centering around the relation of woman to the wage-earning occupations. She was drawn into these through an imperative call, the taking away out of the home of those traditional trades, such as spinning and weaving, which had ceased to be hand work, and had begun to be operated on the machine basis; then into a vast number of new trades, such as office work or paper-box making, springing out of the development of city life, and the unprecedented growth of the means of communication and transportation. Without our railways manufactured goods would accumulate on the hands of the maker and could never reach the customer, near or distant. A certain number of occupations, from time immemorial pursued by men, such as making the cores in foundries, and carpentry and cabinetmaking in furniture factories, are now employing women. All these before any of the recent war developments.

In such ways and many more, women are serving the community; and the community takes the benefits without enquiring too closely what is the cost to the workers. The community has been even slower in comprehending that goods produced by work which is either so cruelly hard or so badly paid that the worker's health and energy are sapped, are sure to prove in the long run a costly indulgence for the community itself. When the purchaser goes into a brightly lighted, well-stocked candy store and pays a dollar or two dollars for a box of chocolate creams, it rarely dawns upon the purchaser, on paying for the confection, that something more than sugar and chocolate has gone into that box, the life force of the young dipper, who in many cases has had to cover one piece every five seconds, for ten hours a day six days a week, and even so has been able to earn but 15 cents an hour. The buyer may not be able to help the girl by paying more for her candy, but she can help her to a larger share of the price by backing trade unions for women, and by insisting on the minimum wage and shorter hours by law.

These lamentable conditions should be brought to an early end. Society must realize how disgraceful, how dangerous it is that so many thousands of women should so spend the promise of their youth in earning five or six dollars a week, that they should toil chilled by cold or exhausted by heat, subjected to the perils of unguarded machinery, to poisonous fumes or to the moral risks that so often attend unlimited overtime or work at night. How can we be content when we know of young waitresses who spend seventy hours a week in striving to please an endless stream of customers?

Again, there are important groups of women who are fulfilling far different functions in the community, the teachers who play year by year a larger part in the upbringing of the next generation, the nurses and attendants who watch over the sick in mind and body, the telephone and telegraph girls who annihilate time and distance for us, the actresses who minister to us our hours of recreation. In every group are some women who are feeling the common impulse to come together, to recognize that an injury to one is the concern of all. Alone, they, too, are unable to handle their peculiar difficulties; and so they are coming to know that their cause is one with that of the poorest paid and most unskilled. If our democracy is to be the real democracy, it must afford scope to human development in every form, and for this end, the right to organize and make the collective bargain must be conceded. There are now teachers' associations affiliated with the American Federation of Labor, several locals of hospital attendants, and a large organization of telephone operators.

A common social inconsistency is seen in the laudation of motherhood, and the supposed value laid upon motherhood as a social and patriotic function. In itself, this stressing of woman's special work for the future is perfectly just; only it so often ends there. If motherhood, a healthy and intelligent motherhood, be woman's unique contribution to the body politic, then common sense would declare that whatever unfits the young girl or the mature woman for future or present maternal duties is at all costs to be prevented. We have no lack of evidence that overwork of women, and the underpay both of men and women themselves and of men who have families to support, is the direct cause both of the loss of little babies, and of the death of mothers in the very act of giving life.

THE FACTS

1: Women are in industry in large numbers and are entering new trades.

2: They work too often under inhuman conditions.

3: For the most part they are unorganized and have only just acquired the power of the vote. Colored women in many of the southern states are still practically voteless.

4: Not only do they suffer from overwork and underpay, but working under such disadvantages, they necessarily become underbidders to men, and seriously weaken what ought to be the solid front of organized labor.

5: As the mothers of the race, they are being injured in regard to this function.

Much can be accomplished in releasing women from such inhuman slavery, by the efforts of trade union women backed by labor men and by those men and women outside of the labor movement to whom has been vouchsafed a knowledge of the facts and sympathy with those who suffer under such evils and maladjustments.

It is usually admitted that human beings are what they are by reason of their ability to think and feel, and that it is through the exercise of that power that progress takes

INTRODUCTION   xiii

place. But our industries are mostly run upon the supposition that the dead material is everything, and the living, breathing human being's interests and welfare are of secondary importance. The trade union views matters differently, and lays stress upon the importance of the human element, and upon all that is best in the human element. It sees in wages not the mere price of so many hours' labor, to be spent in the purchase of food, clothing and shelter, but the means through which freedom of mind, education, home and the very joy of life is to be won and held. In overtime there is the risk to life and health, the increased danger of accident, the lessened resistance to disease, the blotting out of any possibility of growth for the higher faculties, which work has numbed and cramped.

The trade union is a school wherein no one lives unto herself. The members learn to consider every question from the point of view of the general good; they have often to compromise, to balance the lesser advantage against the greater. They have to make important decisions and abide by the results. They appreciate the benefits of co-operative effort, and the futility of individual struggle against economic and social forces. They acquire a practical knowledge of labor legislation as it works out, and can offer useful suggestions as to its improvement. Therefore is the trade union, backed as it is by the whole labor movement, a powerful protection for the woman worker, ensuring her shorter hours, higher wages and a larger share of industrial freedom. The girl who graduates from this school is prepared to accept the new responsibilities of citizenship, which are fast coming to all women. Besides carrying a contribution of value into that larger public life, every group of trade union women exerts a powerful influence upon its unorganized fellow workers; while as voters they present to legislators a certain concrete expression of what is desired by the best type of woman worker, both in industrial matters and in many questions of civic life, such as city government and school affairs. The very difficulties with which we are surrounded should afford us a larger perspective, and stimulate our every effort. Around the nucleus of the trades which have partly organized their women, like the sewing trades, there is the vast army of the unskilled who know no trade union, the packers and the pickers, the carriers of burdens, the counters of change, the bundle girls, the domestic servants, the women in the canneries, in the cotton fields, in the cranberry swamps. Many of these are non-English-speaking foreign women, others are colored women, alike in their industrial loneliness, in their helplessness, in the exploitation from which they suffer.

The submissive qualities which long centuries of economic dependence have engrained into woman's being were a fatal heritage to her when she entered modern industry as a wage-earner. It meant that girls gave in to exaction after exaction; they became, without intending it, the underbidders of men; they have been used to break strikes, and to lower the standards of life, both for themselves and for entire trades. But educate her through the trade union to know the meaning of speeding up, the reason that she must not accept uncomplainingly every cut in wages, and the devotion that she has shown in her individual and family relations will take on a wider meaning, and in loyalty to her fellows she can display a larger unselfishness and a nobler patriotism.

The trade agreement with the employer is ever the best channel for making complaints or suggesting improvements. Through that method, all girls can speak and be heard when the individual worker is voiceless and dumb.

The trade union is a training school in the finer virtues.

INTRODUCTION

The trade union woman grows in intelligence, because in her dealings with her employers she learns to know herself as part of a larger movement. She acquires greater patience, because she has the opportunity of learning what some of her employer's difficulties are.

Great have been the changes of the last few years in every corner of the field of industry, and no group has been more vitally affected by these changes than the women wage-earners.

With the fuller development of industry, the tendency has been to draw women into many occupations and into many processes hitherto considered the domain of men. This tendency was accelerated by the exigencies of the war, when arsenals and machinery plants were filled with women and girls, when elevators were first run by women, railway cars first washed by women; and all this often in defiance of preconceived ideas of what was woman's work. The coming of peace has not meant altogether the slipping back to the old divisions of labor, although it has meant very serious dislocation of industry, and great confusion, both in the rearranging of plants, and in the rearranging of lives, nor is the difficulty at an end.

Almost all the industrial occupations into which women of recent years have made their way are organizable trades; in that they are trades in which there already exists a trade union, and therefore the women at once become of importance to the labor movement, seen as either possible present underbidders, or possible future trade union members.

Further, there are the occupations in which women have been engaged for years, into which the spirit of organization has only very lately begun to creep. These are the occupations in which are found the girls at the switchboard, the women in the schoolhouse, the performers on the stage, and the employes of the Government.

The standardizing by law of wages and hours has made considerable advance during the last ten years. This is chiefly needed by the unorganized women in the poorer trades; but it is backed everywhere by trade unionists without whose aid such legislation would have been almost impossible of attainment. The establishment of the Women's Bureau is in itself an achievement of no small importance, and can be credited to women, especially the women of the trade unions, supported by trade union men and by women's clubs, and other sympathetic organizations.

The political enfranchisement of women has coincided with the industrial changes and undoubtedly has greatly strengthened the position of the wage-earning woman, whether trade unionist or non-trade unionist, and will strengthen it still further when in course of years the new voters learn how to make full use of this as yet unfamiliar tool.

Women are being caught up by the movement for education, and numerous are the requests they make for information as to their rights and responsibilities. Nor do all of these requests come from women. Men, too, in great number are realizing that these co-workers of theirs are here to stay. Being here to stay, it is desirable that they should be partners in industry upon an honorable and self-respecting footing.

The status of women has up to the present been one of the most unsatisfactory elements in the labor question. Into one trade after another have women been pitchforked. Training was the last thing they were expected to need, unless indeed that was wages. Only a long and weary fight has brought about for a selected few better pay and shorter hours. The rest are still the underbidders of men, overworked, underpaid, and too often killed or wrecked in their early womanhood before the very eyes of a society too

INTRODUCTION

stupid to value aright the life of a young girl or a young mother.

But whispers come to us, whispers of discontent in quarters where it was least expected, and when the dumb start speaking, they have unexpected things to tell us.

Although the aim here is to trace woman's connection with the labor movement as herself an active worker, women have in the past continually strengthened the labor movement indirectly through their support of the men of their families; this is seen most markedly in strikes, lockouts and long periods of unemployment. They have sometimes borne the hardest share because the men at least had some power of decision and could exert themselves, if they had power of leadership, in leading others. For the women, there was nothing left but endurance, endurance of the poverty that comes in the train of every industrial struggle, that strips home of its little comforts, that often brings sickness and even death into the home. It is the same now for the wives of the miners in the strike-affected districts where unionism is still taboo. The wives of the striking shopmen in many a railway center are today, through this very endurance and loyal support of their men, making a notable contribution towards the strength of the labor movement.

There have been also a few women like Mother Jones, who, although they have not contributed specially towards the strengthening of the labor movement among women, have proved themselves notable leaders of men's groups.

CONTENTS

		PAGE
PREFACE		vii
INTRODUCTION		ix

CHAPTER

I	PRIMITIVE WOMAN IN INDUSTRY	23
II	THE COLONIAL WOMAN	31
III	WOMEN AND MACHINE INDUSTRY	37
IV	WOMEN IN SOME MODERN TRADE UNIONS	57
V	WOMEN IN SOME MODERN TRADE UNIONS (continued)	85
VI	A NEW DEVELOPMENT IN ORGANIZATION—THE WOMEN'S TRADE UNION LEAGUE	106
VII	INDUSTRIAL LEGISLATION	123
VIII	THE MINIMUM WAGE	143
IX	THE WOMEN'S BUREAU	166
X	WORKING WOMEN AND THE WAR	186
XI	THE NEGRO WOMAN	202
XII	INTERNATIONAL FEDERATION OF WORKING WOMEN	212
XIII	CONCLUSION	229
	SOURCE LIST OF REFERENCES AND READING	232
	INDEX	235

WOMEN AND THE LABOR MOVEMENT

WOMEN AND THE LABOR MOVEMENT

Chapter I

PRIMITIVE WOMAN IN INDUSTRY

For many years scientific men have been studying the more primitive peoples, and have thrown much light upon those early forefathers of the race. The geologist has found among the rocks faint traces of human existence. The archaeologist has collected crude tools and garments, remnants of early homes, and records clear for him to read, of their culture. In these researches woman and her doings have not been entirely overlooked. Even as far back as the Roman historians we find evidence that woman's share in those early beginnings of civilization was too important to be ignored. Still it is only lately, however, that woman's part in the making of the world of that day and in the preparing of the world as we know it now in our day, has received close and careful attention. There is still a great deal of work to be done before so vast a field can be thoroughly explored.

A small group of scientists has of recent years laid special emphasis upon primitive woman, and through their researches and writings we are now able to build up a fairly clear picture of how great is the debt owed to her.

The first, as far as I know, among writers in the English

language, to draw attention to the discoveries and the achievements of those early creators of civilization was Otis T. Mason, in "Woman's Share in Primitive Culture," published in 1894, and still referred to as an authority. Mr. Mason shows how extensive and unceasing were the labors of the women of those early times, and how successful they were in utilizing the crude materials at their hand, for the support of their families and for the enriching of life.

With wealth of illustration he has recorded and interpreted for us their achievements as food bringers, weavers and basket-makers, their skill in turning the skins of animals to good purpose, in making the first clay vessels to hold food, or to be transformed into things of beauty by some primitive magic of decoration, for they were artists too. Women were the first linguists; they were, even in those early days, the founders of society and its conservators.

Otis T. Mason has been followed by such investigators as William I. Thomas, Lester F. Ward, Thorstein B. Veblen, John M. Tyler, Elsie Worthington Parsons, while Charlotte Perkins Gilman, Catherine Gasquoine Gallichan and others have popularized much of the same material.

Writers may differ profoundly as to the degree of women's importance and power in the society of their day in prehistoric and early historic times, but they are unanimous in according to average woman the credit for being the mother of the arts, the pioneer in culture and the architect of the pristine community. The man in those early days was, it is agreed, a much simpler being than his mate. He wandered far afield in search of game or in pursuit of his foes. On the surface, one would say that he was the adventurous one. But with hunting and fighting he reached the limit of his adventures. It was woman, apparently so tied down and limited by the claims of her children, who after all was to find fullest scope for her energies. In that day to stay at home was to be the inventor, the discoverer, the teacher, the leader. Fison and Howitt (quoted by many authorities) put it most tersely when they say, speaking of the Australian aborigines, "A man hunts, spears fish and sits about. All the rest is woman's work." Thorstein Veblen, speaking generally, expresses it thus: "Fighting, together with other work that involves a serious element of exploration, becomes the employment of the able-bodied men; the uneventful everyday work of the group falls to the woman and the infirm."

As long as the man had to expend most of his energies in such exhausting pursuits as hunting and fighting, he was compelled to rest, to idle during his hours or days near the primitive fireside. Meanwhile women were becoming of constantly increasing value to men because they were producers.

Woman's work might on the whole be just as hard, but she did not have to expend her energy so violently and within such brief periods, so that she had more time and more thought to give to those domestic arts, which she pursued for the sake of her man and her children. Motherhood was the great teacher. For the infant the mother exerted all her powers of invention, all her quickness and resourcefulness in utilizing what she found to her hand.

Professor Thomas ("Sex and Society") points out that one of the most remarkable and unexpected results of woman's performance of the great function of home-maker was not only to make of her, as we have shown, the first weaver, the first artificer, the first artist, the first gardener. This had another reaction, one quite as important; it made of her a more highly developed being, a being socially more advanced and far fitter for her high task, the training of children, and the advancing if by ever so little of the next generation on the path toward civilization. She had more or less to associate together with her fellow-women and with the growing children and therefore she rose in culture.

While much of the knowledge that we have gained about primitive woman comes from digging into the remote past, let us not forget that primitive woman exists still, although at a somewhat advanced stage of culture. Many inferences drawn from the silent record of the past have been checked, interpreted and confirmed by the observations of explorers and travelers. A few instances of these will illustrate what is meant. They are the more striking because they are taken from peoples widely separated, and not at all akin. MacDonald thus describes the customs of East Central Africa: "The work is done chiefly by the women. This is universal. They hoe the fields, sow the seed and reap the harvest. To them too falls the labor of house building, grinding corn, brewing beer, cooking, washing and caring for all the material interests of the community. The men tend the cattle, hunt, go to war; they also spend much time sitting in council over the conduct of affairs." Mrs. Gallichan ("The Age of Mother-Power") tells how one traveler saw the women in the Pelew Islands as the agriculturists of the tribe:

In the Pelew Islands women are most important because they work the taro fields. The richest woman in the village looks with pride on her taro patch, and although she has female followers enough to allow her to merely superintend the work without taking part in it, she nevertheless prefers to lay aside her fine apron and to betake herself to the field, merely clad in a small apron that barely hides her nakedness with a little mat on her back to protect her from the boiling heat of the sun, and with a shade of banana leaves for her eyes. There, dripping with sweat in the burning sun, and coated with mud to the hips and down to the

PRIMITIVE WOMAN IN INDUSTRY

elbow, she toils to set the younger woman a good example. Moreover, as in every other occupation, the kalitho, the gods, must be invoked and who could be better fitted for the discharge of so important a duty as the mother of the house?

Thorstein Veblen in his "Instinct of Workmanship," in speaking of the beginnings of agriculture, dwells upon woman's innate liking for and interest in young growing things.

Now, as has already been said, the scheme of life of the crops and flocks is, at least in the main, and particularly so far as it vitally and always interests their keepers, a scheme of fecundity, fertility and growth. But these matters visibly and by conscious sentiment, pertain in a peculiarly intimate sense to the woman. They are matters in which the sympathetic insight and fellow feeling of womankind should in the nature of things come very felicitously to further the propitious course of things. Besides which, the life of the woman falls in these same lines of fecundity, nature and growth, so that their association and attendance on the flocks and groups should further the propitious course of things, also by the subtler means of sympathetic suggestion.

Tyler ("New Stone Age in Northern Europe") leads up to women's importance in agriculture. The evidence of that period shows the women as the inventors and discoverers of the household crafts as well as most of our science. Because they were the first herbalists, they were the first household physicians. In the care of children they were compelled to be alert, quick minded, ready for all sorts of emergencies.

The woman provided the vegetable food as well as much of the animal, and became the first gardener and farmer. She introduced tillage of the ground, and thus became economically by far the more important member of the partnership, and she probably had by far the more alert, quick-witted brain.

Further, the establishment of agriculture gave rise to the idea of the earth mother. Savage man inclines to eat the seed corn so there is none to carry over to the next season. It has been difficult, therefore, to introduce agriculture among savage peoples, especially among nomadic tribes. The early women agriculturists are supposed to have established the idea of the taboo of the goddess. Though man would not control his appetites so as to save the corn for planting, he did yield to the supernatural warning. The planting of crops became possible and this in the end led to the regular settlement.

Robert H. Lowie in "Primitive Society" analyzes very carefully the great amount of material that has been brought together by various travelers, and interpreted by men of science. He urges the greatest caution in theorizing too loosely where our information is necessarily so incomplete. He shows that division of labor between the sexes is often a conventional thing. The Bantu races in Africa do not permit women to attend to the herd; whereas Hottentot women are the regular milkers. He goes on:—

> The treatment of women is one thing, her legal status another; her opportunities for public activities still another, while the character and extent of her labors belong again to a distinct category.

He thinks that plain borrowing of customs is a frequent reason for the finding of similar practices over wide regions of the earth's surface. How else, he says, can we account for the ceremonial and habitual separation of the sexes as found, in its extremest form in the Islands of the Pacific, but in a degree, characteristic of the early inhabitants of the entire Pacific Coast of North America.

Lowie quotes from Bogoras his account of the manner of living of different tribes of the Chukchi, a people like the

Eskimo. They were a maritime community, and the women took little active part in the earning of the living, but apparently led a comparatively easy and non-productive life. When the reindeer was introduced among them a change took place, the women of reindeer-owning tribes leading a harder life. They had, however, become economically more useful, and therefore had a better prospect of an independent existence.

In the long last the real importance of any individual is in proportion to his or her usefulness to the community. No one will deny that the early mothers of the race were of a supreme value to their fellows. What we call today the parasitic woman was unknown. The parasitic woman is of two kinds, it is true. She who openly lives for enjoyment and is of use to no mortal being, and the other, far more common, who simply has no place in life, is supported by some man and does nothing useful or worthwhile in return, as for instance an unmarried daughter living at home and doing nothing in particular.

It seems desirable to link up the modern industrial woman with her far past ancestress. It is indeed with a sense of pride that we working women of today can look back to her. Like us, she worked, worked incessantly, but also, unlike some of us, she was a pioneer and a leader, inventing and progressing, even though her progress was probably invisible to herself and only to be detected in the long perspective of ages.

Rudyard Kipling, in "The Cat That Walked by Himself," gives a vivid and dramatic picture of primitive woman's resourcefulness, although the particular achievement he chooses with which to make his point, the taming of animals, happens to lie in a field now generally assigned to man. He is perhaps closer to the truth in his reading of the past, when he credits early woman with being an agent in the process of taming man himself. As the vision of the writer sees it, "Of course the man was dreadfully wild till he met the woman, and she told him that she did not like living in his wild ways. She picked out a nice dry cave, instead of a heap of wild leaves to lie down on; and she strewed clean sand on the floor; and she lit a nice wood fire at the back of the cave; and she hung a dried wild horse skin, tail down, across the opening of the cave; and she said 'Wipe your feet, dear, when you come in, and now we will keep house.'"

CHAPTER II

THE COLONIAL WOMAN

If primitive woman is to us an inspiration and an encouragement, an example different but no less interesting is set us moderns by the colonial woman of our own country. Although on a very different level of culture and in a far advanced stage of civilization, the colonial woman, too, was the domestic producer, pursuing many of the very same historic trades. As in primitive days, the home of colonial times was essentially a productive institution and the center of the productive life of the community. Because of its economic importance everything in woman's life centered around the home, and was planned with reference to it. In those early days there was no setting aside of useless rooms; all the spare house space was utilized by the industry that had to be carried on within it. The home was by no means merely a place to live in. It was also a place in which very largely the living was earned, and the goods produced that were to be consumed by the little group within. If anyone wishes to see life in a form something like what it was lived before the Revolution, he may travel now into the remote mountain regions of Kentucky, Tennessee, Georgia and the Carolinas. Beyond where the railroads have run out into dead ends in the little valleys far away from modern life, there still live the descendants of the early colonial settlers of those regions. Year by year the old life is disappearing, as schools, improved roads and better methods of marketing are introduced. But we have a proof of the tenacity with which the home industries and domestic production have maintained themselves in the southern mountains in that the products of these very industries, as organized through the mountain schools, are put upon the market of our cities today.

In the various communities that grew up on the Atlantic coast, in the New England colonies, in the Pennsylvania region as well as in the southern settlements, there were extremely primitive standards of living, much more primitive, and lasting on to a much later period, than in Great Britain itself. For this there were a number of reasons. The country, so recently settled, lacked many improvements, and the home many conveniences in use in the older countries of Europe. Another reason why pioneer conditions of living and of housekeeping still persisted, was that the industrial revolution had not yet touched them. The age of machine industry had for America not yet begun. These changes were in full swing in England, and had already profoundly affected the life of the people and the trade and commerce of the country before the period of the War of Independence. During the disturbed years that followed the North American colonies remained almost entirely agricultural; the population still very small, with next to no roads, the best methods of transport being by boat on the rivers, or between the larger coast towns by seagoing vessels. The towns themselves (they were hardly cities) were at that time only six: Boston, Salem, New York, Philadelphia, Baltimore and Charleston. They had no streets as we know streets, merely roads full of dust in summer, and mud, snow and ice in the winter, with no water supply and no sewerage system, and of course no methods of street lighting.

Therefore, it is evident that living in a town, the woman of that day had to perform for her family many tasks which

THE COLONIAL WOMAN

today she is saved by the municipality or manufacturer. In the country the wife and daughters of the farmers had, even in a greater degree than the town-dwelling woman, abundance of work provided for them. The country home, and most homes were country homes, was quite a self-contained community in itself. On the farm were raised the sheep whose fleece was to keep the family warm through the long cold winters. In the fields grew the flax out of which were woven the linen tablecloths and sheets and clothing. The cattle or sheep and even more commonly the pig, bred by the farmer and by him turned into meat, was handed over to his wife and daughters to prepare for the table and to salt down for future use. The women of the family utilized the spare fat to make soap and candles. The wool of the sheep they had to cleanse and comb in preparation for spinning. The spinning wheel was always ready at hand for the industrious spinner. Weaving of the lighter materials was a somewhat more complicated process, but equally part of the woman's work. In order to satisfy her eye for color the early colonial woman had learned to make use of vegetable dyes made from plants gathered in the woods.

Even silk, it is related, was manufactured on American soil in the time of the very earliest settlers from cocoons sent over by King James the First.

From this it is easy to see that little ready money was needed in those days. The women of the household produced much of what was needed to satisfy family requirements, and in those simple days but little was purchased from the outside.

These family needs met, the women turned to earning extra money by either selling the product of their spinning looms to a village store, or else weaving cloth or it may be knitting stockings to order for individual customers.

This was domestic production upon a perfectly sound economic basis. It is not to be confused with the wasteful and injurious methods of home work among ourselves today. The early colonial woman undoubtedly worked hard; she had to submit to many privations, but the privations were mostly of the unavoidable sort which, so long as they are seen to be unavoidable, courageous humanity bears unmurmuringly. In addition the domestic producer of those days was very much her own mistress. She could plan her work as best suited her. Her daughters were her helpers in contributing to the family income, while the maids of the household, very likely the daughters of the neighboring farmers, were much on a position of equality with the girls of the household. In performing their share of the household industry they were serving an apprenticeship to what was going to be a valuable trade for them when they left for homes of their own. The habitual reckoning of the income as family income accurately describes women's relation to money. In those days the father was in every sense the head of the house, and it was he who had control of the common purse. On the other hand, the arrangement was, for those days, not an unfair one. Woman's contribution to the household consisted of her share of all the activities that made for support and comfort, and she had in return shelter, food and clothing, and there was very little else for anyone then. The men of the home did the rougher, more exposed, and in most cases more dangerous work out of doors. They felled the forests, built the roads and made the journeys on family business, planted the fields and cared for the cattle.

As life became easier, we can observe the first beginnings of the factory system. This was merely the opening of large rooms where a business man would install a large number of hand looms. Sometimes the yarn would be delivered

THE COLONIAL WOMAN

there by the home spinner. About this time we hear much of spinning schools, encouraged for the purpose of teaching women to spin. Unfortunately there was an equal eagerness to turn children, both girls and boys, into spinners and helpers, for great was the anxiety to convert the children's labor into profit, and this usually on the ground that their work would add materially to the wealth of the country and also it would save the children themselves all the evil effects of a life of idleness. Miss Edith Abbott ("Women in Industry"), quoting from original documents, shows that this approval of child labor was universal and that early inventors actually worked to discover possible means of using the labor of children. Indeed a little later on, early in the next century, commendation was solicited for one machine on the ground that it could be turned by children from five to ten years of age.

The first really commercial enterprises that women pursued were such as the keeping of small shops and of inns. Of these Miss Abbott gives an interesting account. Some women only got a license to keep a tavern on condition that they had a careful man to manage the house. However, widows often took up this business. The prosecution of one woman in New Haven casts a light, anything but creditable, on the methods of her business management, because of her systematic overcharging, giving details that have a familiar modern ring in it as that "she sold a piece of cloth to the two Mecars at 23s 4d per yard in wompom; the cloth cost her about 12s per yard and sold when wompom was in great request."

The raising of garden seeds was something very natural for women to engage in as a business, seeing that from the earliest times in the Colonies they had had the charge of whatever kitchen garden was attached to their own home. Women were teachers of dames' schools. Of course there were nurses and midwives. There are occasional instances of women carrying on real industrial establishments. Instances cited are mills, saw-mills and even a slaughter house. A few women were bakers and quite a number were printers, both compositors and working at the press.

CHAPTER III

WOMEN AND MACHINE INDUSTRY

Meanwhile the development of the factory system with its introduction of power-driven machinery was preparing the way for a complete change in the industrial system of the United States. A series of inventions had led up to the creation of the machine-driven industry that was so soon to be transplanted from British to American soil. In its turn, but not yet. The country in which this gigantic experiment was first tried out, Great Britain, gained in the form of an enormously increased production, of a foreign trade never before matched in the world's history, in an extension of colonial markets equally unprecedented. For all these benefits England paid a dear price: the herding of the workers into cities, the carrying on of their labors for inhuman hours under insanitary conditions, for poor pay, and with an appalling sacrifice of child life and child happiness, and the sapping of the vitality of her people. Too many of these errors were to be repeated by the United States, but at the time when this country enthusiastically welcomed the introduction of machinery into industry, the wheel had not yet come full circle and machines were set up in the newly established textile mills without a single misgiving.

The textile industry was the mother industry wherein machinery was first adopted. The mechanical improvements which revolutionized the making of woven goods were the steam engine, the spinning jenny, the power loom and the cotton gin. The steam engine, when applied to the driving of a loom, multiplied enormously the power of the human hand in producing cloth, and the mechanism was christened a power loom. Two other inventions made it possible to keep this all-devouring machine supplied with yarn for conversion into the finished article. One of these, though the later to be put upon the market, was the cotton gin, which did away with the need for picking out by hand the seeds from the raw cotton. The spinning jenny was proportionately efficient in producing yarn ready for weaving.

The setting up of these various machines meant the sinking of much capital. It meant that they had to be housed in specially built factories, and the owners, usually a body of stockholders, had to have capital to employ a staff of workers to operate the machines.

Textile machinery had been invented and manufactured in England, and there were easily understandable objections to the operating of such machines elsewhere and objections to the emigration of the skilled employes accustomed to running them. It was not till after the close of the war of 1812 that these difficulties passed away and in the year 1814 the first power loom was erected on American soil at Waltham, Massachusetts. The name of the first young woman weaver who took her place in command of this marvelous new invention was Deborah Skinner. It is recorded that in 1817 there were three power looms in Fall River, Massachusetts. The names of the girl weavers were Sallie Winters, Hannah Borden and Mary Healy.

Hannah Borden, we are told, was an expert hand weaver when quite a little girl. Her father being one of the stockholders in the Fall River mill, found an opening for her. Her position was typical of that of her entire generation. They were pioneers in a new form of industry. As pioneers they sacrificed nothing of their established social position in the little community; they were in touch with the church life and the culture, the reading and the literary interests. On the other hand, they submitted to conditions that we have learned to think utterly wrong today. They worked from sunrise till seven or half past seven in the evening, even weaving by candle light in the winter nights. Wages are recorded as from $2.75 to $3.25 a week. Although Hannah Borden herself was under no compulsion to speed up her work, the managers being only too pleased with the profits she and her fellows were making for them, running one loom apiece, these first workers were nevertheless unthinkingly accepting a new creed in industry which they themselves were soon to resent and for which generations after them were to suffer.

The factory employes of that day were all American born, so there could be no jealousy between workers of rival races, nor could one group of workers be played off against another.

Mills increased in numbers, mill owners prospered and presently the number of girls coming in from the country districts to work all of the year or part of the year became so great that there was no accommodation for them. The mill owners then proceeded to erect boarding houses, with a fixed rate of payment per lodger, guaranteed to the boarding-house keeper. There was no worship of fresh air in those days nor were there any public health officers, or the ventilation of the mills and the overcrowding of the boarding houses would have given grounds for investigation. One description that has come down to us speaks of the boarding houses as being absolutely blocked with articles of furniture, umbrellas, boxes and clothing. It is not therefore surprising that under these circumstances there was a great prevalence of consumption, a disease that had ever been the bane of New England from quite early times. So common was it that families looked upon it as an inevitable curse. We know now that under all the circumstances of the life of those days, the dread of fresh air indoors was such as to give the sick small chance for recovery and the well every chance for becoming infected.

The making of shoes was another industry into which woman entered early. Her labor was utilized when the towns became large enough to maintain regular cobblers' shops. The cobblers divided up the work, sending out the uppers to be stitched and the shoes to be bound by women. It is said to have been a well paid trade, and was like modern home work in that a great many married women worked at it as a side occupation in the intervals of their house work. Shoe-making as an industry in machine-equipped factories developed much later and was later still in attracting women into it.

We are accustomed to think of tobacco as the crop, even if its manufacture into commercial tobacco is not always the industry of the warm southern states. But if people want a luxury, and cannot obtain it elsewhere, they manage to procure some sort of substitute, so the colonial farmers and their wives raised a crude tobacco on their northern fields, and cigar making was an occupation of women in the early years of this century until better tobacco from the south and better cigar makers from other countries produced a more delicate and highly finished article.

The earliest information that we have about women's trade unions dates back to the year 1825, although men, it is said, had become active earlier. The first American women factory workers were of a blood and of a race that it was not easy to suppress, and the newspapers of that year record some tailoresses turning out for higher wages. As the years went on more tailoresses struck. In 1831,

1,600 women struck for a wage scale, with Miss Louisa M. Mitchell as Secretary of the Tailoresses' Society, Mrs. Lavinia Waight being President.

The seamstresses and tailoresses of Baltimore formed an organization in 1833. In this they were supported by the journeymen tailors. The poor wages and bad conditions of the sewing women must have attracted public attention for Mr. Booth, the great actor, was announced as giving a performance for the benefit of the Seamstresses' Society.

It was in 1828 that Mathew Carey, an independent and public-spirited citizen, began to call attention to the low wages paid to the working women in Philadelphia. In 1835 he presided over a large meeting of Philadelphia Working Women, at the request of a committee of 18 women. This committee included representatives of many branches of the sewing trade. They formed an association called "The Female Improvement Society" which was actually a city federation of working women's organizations. They submitted wage scales to the employers, secured newspaper publicity, and sent a protest to the Secretary of War against the low prices paid for army orders. It was stated that most of the employers seem to have granted a slight advance in wages.

It was in the cotton mills of New England, however, that occurred most of the larger strikes which attracted publicity to the industry, and did something towards checking its increasingly burdensome exactions. In the year 1828 there was a large strike of cotton mill operatives in Dover, New Hampshire, the news of which the papers spread from Maine to Georgia. In Paterson, New Jersey, too, there was even a strike, beginning among the children, which presently extended to the carpenters, masons and machinists, who united in demanding a ten hour day.

A yet larger strike occurred six years later, in Dover,

New Hampshire, which turned on the question of a reduction in wages. In this struggle the girls held meetings, passed resolutions and made use of the press, where editors were favorable, to spread the news through New Hampshire and as far as Lowell in Massachusetts. It was inferred that the Dover girls had taken example by those of Lowell in going out on strike and forming a trade union, for the same unrest prevailed in Lowell, a much larger city. With the vivacity and spirit for which the Lowell girls were noted, they issued a proclamation and attracted public attention to the announcement of their wrongs. This time the strikebreaker was on their track, a large number of girls from the surrounding country coming in to Lowell with a view of filling the strikers' places.

In 1836, in Lowell, the housekeepers of the boarding houses arranged with the mill-owners to raise their price ($1.25 per week) by 24 cents; one-half to be paid by the girl, the other deducted from her pay and handed over to the housekeeper. There was then something like a trade union, so the girls struck, and went out to the number of twenty-five hundred. The strike ended in defeat, but it attracted the attention of the men at the annual convention of the National Trade Union, when in the report on female labor, women were recommended to "immediately adopt energetic measures, in the construction of societies, to support each other."

There was so little continuity in the labor movement of that day that, although under the pressure of poverty and overwork, strike after strike took place, one organization and another came to life, only to exist a little while, thus leaving the workers no better off.

Exactly similar stories are told of Philadelphia and Norristown, Pennsylvania, of Amesbury and Springfield, Massachusetts, of Baltimore and New York. There were other trades involved besides cotton weaving, umbrella sewing, tailoring, book binding and shoe binding.

The shoe binders had in Lynn a well-organized union called "The Female Society of Lynn and Vicinity for the Protection and Promotion of Female Industry." For a while this society was extremely successful and was so influential that it appointed two delegates (men) to represent them at the Boston Central Labor Body. Unfortunately six months saw this promising union in difficulties. Since there is nothing heard of it after that, it probably went out of existence very soon.

Outside of working women we know of one woman who exercised remarkable influence wherever she moved. This was Frances Wright. Born in Scotland in 1795 she soon became an orphan and at the same time heir to a great deal of property. She early became imbued with the ideas of French writers of the liberal school, and came to this country in 1818, feeling that she was leaving an effete old world for a new land full of promise. Returning to her home she again sailed for America in 1825, purchased a large tract of land in Tennessee within a few miles of where Memphis now stands, and established there a colony of freed slaves. Her work there came to an end because she found herself checkmated by the laws of the state regarding Negroes. The colonists were sent safely to Haiti.

Later we find her associated with Robert Dale Owen. She became a writer and a public lecturer, traveling throughout the western states attacking slavery and other established social institutions and advocating the freeing of women from political and economic handicaps. Her keen intellect saw even so early that the hope of the working classes lay in organized labor. She is quoted in Commons' "Documentary History of American Industrial Society"— "It has long been clear to me that in every country the best feeling and the best sense are found with the laboring and useful classes, and the worst sense with the idle and useless; until all classes shall be amalgamated into one, however, by gradual but fundamental changes in the whole organization of society, much bad feeling must prevail everywhere."

Again, of the Working Men's Party in 1833 she wrote "It is labor rising up against idleness, industry against money and against privilege."

It is usual to consider the period from 1840 to 1860 as having a character of its own in the growth of the American labor movement. The thought of some ran along the lines of land reform and co-operation, expressing a certain social idealism. Another movement centered around the efforts made to better the position of working people through organizations officered and managed by themselves, with the sympathetic support of a group of advanced writers and thinkers. There were some very remarkable working women who took part in the meetings of the New England Working Men's Association, later known as the New England Labor Reform League, between 1845 and 1847, also in the National Industrial Congress which met annually until 1855. Dr. Andrews relates how a woman speaker, a working woman, asked direct support for the factory girls, as the men had the ballot box to help them. She said she "wished the members of the legislature might be mill operatives a few weeks, occupy their rooms, and eat at their tables. Then they would know why a thousand of us asked them to protect us."

But if unionism, strictly so called, was in the background and temporarily somewhat inactive, there were strikes a-plenty. In 1851, a successful shirt sewers' co-operative union grew out of an attempt to relieve the necessities of 6,000 shirt sewers in the city of New York. Thomas Hood's

"Song of the Shirt" was quoted to the public as applying to New York as well as to London, for thousands of these women were

> "Sewing at once with a double stitch,
> A shroud as well as a shirt."

The Female Labor Reform Associations, with their neutral title, were none the less trade unions, although they gave less of their attention to forming unions than to legislation. Women were very helpless and had from time to time to face fresh difficulties, such as the arrival in their cities of immigrants who, in order to get a footing, were willing to take any wages. The leaders therefore felt that organization was far too slow a method to reach the evils of constantly lessening wages and the unceasing pressure of work to which the rank and file had to submit. As described elsewhere, their program was to gain a ten hour day for both men and women and to gain it in several states at once. They hoped thus to do away with the supposedly convincing argument used by the Pittsburgh and Allegheny employers that they could not afford to reduce hours or increase wages in the face of the competition of the New England mills. In this, these brave women failed.

Miss Sarah G. Bagley was President of the Lowell Female Labor Reform Association. In 1845 she was sent as a delegate to a Convention of the New England Working Men's Association. She testified before the Massachusetts Legislative Committee as to the conditions in textile mills. Later she and her followers were instrumental in helping to defeat William Schouler, who had been Chairman of the Special Committee of the Legislature, because he had treated with contempt the presentation of their case.

From the Lowell Labor Reform Association, four women

delegates, Mary Emerson, Sarah G. Bagley, Mary H. Carleton and Huldah J. Stone, were seated at the first Industrial Congress at Boston. Out of the ten delegates sent by the New England Labor Reform League to the National Reform Convention at Worcester, three were women, Miss Emerson, Miss Stone and Miss Bagley. All this is clear proof of how very active the women were at this period. At these Conventions there were complaints made of the employment of the black list, which deprived women of the chance of obtaining work in other houses or in other towns.

National Industrial Congresses continued to meet from 1846 to 1855. At the second congress in 1847, Mrs. Fannie Lee Townsend, of Providence, R. I., was seated as an honorary member. She spoke and entered into the discussions on the position of women.

The Labor Reform Associations were in many ways far in advance of any previous efforts made by women. Their leaders had a definite policy to which they adhered; they were women of ability, well fitted to meet either labor men, employers or legislators, in discussion. They understood economics and saw the need for co-operation of the workers so clearly that their interstate campaigns remain a model for us today, conducted as they were under all the difficulties of distance and imperfect means of communication and transportation.

But forces were at work that no heroism or ability or intelligence could counteract. The question of slavery was soon the foremost question of all others. If public interest was entirely absorbed by the war as long as it lasted, and if during that time labor received but scant attention, even worse days were ahead with the coming of peace and the consequent long depression, reaching its climax in the panic of 1873. But labor was not idle. There were eight hour leagues, of which the Boston League, formed in 1869, was

WOMEN AND MACHINE INDUSTRY 47

the first to admit women. There were also more than 30 national trade unions, two of these only, printers and cigar makers, admitting women.

Women shoe makers were very active. There was a strike of several hundred shoe stitchers at Lynn, Massachusetts, in the winter of 1860. They even marched in parade, 5000 men and 1000 women, with music and banners, and held a mass meeting afterwards. The strike resulted in getting some of the demands and in the formation of a shoe makers' union. The women shoe makers had their own National Trade Union, the Daughters of St. Crispin. It is the only women's national organization of which we have record.

At its first convention in 1869, at Lynn, Massachusetts, there were delegates from many of the principal shoe centers in Massachusetts, from Auburn, Maine, Rochester, New York, Philadelphia, Chicago, and even San Francisco. The men had a union called the Knights of St. Crispin, and the Daughters were to do for the women what the Knights' organization was endeavoring to accomplish for the men. The order really came into existence through the support of the organized men, who loyally supported their sisters, going out on strike on behalf of Daughters who had been discharged for belonging to a trade union. This was another of the organizations which succumbed in the hard times of 1873. The training that some of the more active had received while in St. Crispin's fold, they carried over with them when later on they had the opportunity to join the Knights of Labor.

Massachusetts and New York had state unions of working women including women of different grades. The purpose of the Massachusetts State Union was "to procure diminution of the hours of labor in the factories, to ameliorate the condition of the working women generally, and to take steps to form protective organization of all trades," also to encourage women to serve regular apprenticeships.

References to suffrage occur in the labor papers and from the reports of conventions and meetings. The subject evidently frequently came up for discussion, but even among the working women, only a few had yet been converted to see the need for the vote.

Under other names and over the larger territory extending to the cities of the middle west, the industrial struggle continued. The textile mills were now full of immigrant workers. They were even less fitted than the Lowell girls had been to face the increasing hardships of their position. It is encouraging to note one most successful strike of weavers, men and women, but led by the women, who decided to limit their attack to three mills only, and go on working in the others, meanwhile soliciting contributions toward the strike fund throughout the eastern states. They gave the managers every opportunity to lock them out, so that upon the manufacturers might fall the onus of breaking their contracts to their customers. Three thousand two hundred and fifteen strikers were on the unions' payroll. After lasting about two months, the strike was successful.

The Working Women's Protective Union, begun in 1866, was still in operation twenty-seven years afterwards, for it was reported upon for the World's Fair in 1893. Its special work was the collection of wages which women could not collect for themselves. Its managers, however, found themselves quite unable to help the girls in a matter that was just as much a wage question, although not generally considered so. That was to check the fining system, or to secure any refund of fines. The union was also an agency for obtaining employment for women. There were similar associations in Boston, Philadelphia, Chicago, St. Louis, Indianapolis and elsewhere.

The Working Women's Association of New York was

WOMEN AND MACHINE INDUSTRY

another organization organized by non-working women, leaders in the woman suffrage movement. The majority of working women were not at that time interested in the vote, and the suffragists' appeal for co-operative action to obtain the vote as an instrument to improve industrial conditions fell flat.

The International Workingmen's Association, from 1866 to 1873, is considered by Dr. John B. Andrews as having been a radical influence in American labor unionism. "Women," he added, "were admitted as members, the word 'workingmen' being understood in its broad meaning to include both sexes, but the organization aside from its educational influence may be disregarded as a factor in the development of women's trade unions." According to the "Documentary History of American Industrial Society" the one woman whose name is closely associated with its activities in this country was Victoria Woodhull, although her connection had an uneasy close. In the American branch, with which the trade unions of the United States had been asked to affiliate, charges were brought against Section 12, which Mrs. Woodhull dominated, that it was introducing issues foreign to the labor question, such as woman suffrage, free love, a universal language, and so on. Both factions appealed to the Convention of the International, when it met at the Hague, and the Convention ruled against Section 12. A resolution was adopted that no section hereafter be admitted which did not consist of at least three-fourths of wage laborers.

For a short time, also, Mrs. Woodhull was very prominent as a free lance, in the woman suffrage movement. She must have been a woman of brilliant ability, but also an individualist who forged ahead by herself, and was a little impatient, doubtless, of the dull routine of gathering together and winning over to her plans any considerable group of followers.

The Knights of Labor, an organization planned on a national scale, and coming to the front during the latter third of the nineteenth century, was for a time probably the chief labor influence in the United States. Certainly during the few brief years of its greatest activity it did much to forward the cause of the working woman. It was a large body, and very informally organized; at first a secret order, altruistic in its aims and middle class in its membership. At its first convention in 1878 it was reorganized, and from then on began to draw in the workers in the trades, as well as housekeeping women and farmers. Although a number of its locals, especially among the shoe workers, were composed solely of those of one trade and usually also of one sex, that was not the general rule. The locals were, broadly speaking, on the federal labor union pattern, but even more flexible, including all who would support the main principle, "That is the most perfect government in which an injury to one is the concern of all." Those who followed occupations which were considered as in opposition to such a creed were excluded; these were lawyers, bankers, stock brokers, dealers in intoxicating liquors and professional gamblers. Their leaders perceived clearly that the uncertain position of women in the labor movement was one that was fraught with much suffering to themselves and great danger to the men wage earners, and therefore the first regular constitution of the reorganized Knights of Labor included as one of the objects "to secure equal pay for equal work."

This subject was often afterwards referred to, and in 1881, women were admitted to regular membership. For almost the first time it now becomes possible to follow closely what happened in the history of an organization, as the records of conventions of the Knights of Labor are printed, and obtainable in many libraries.

There were reports on women's work and addresses to the membership. The convention of 1886 appointed Leonora M. Barry as general investigator, and for four years she conducted almost single handed, except for the help of her secretary, Mary O'Reilly, a most remarkable campaign on behalf of the woman wage earner. Unofficially she inspected factories until she found that helpless girls whom she had interviewed even privately, were often in consequence discharged. Thus she helped to pave the way for the state labor departments of today. A brilliant and effective speaker, she roused the women of the leisure classes in the women's clubs and suffrage associations. She organized many locals and is heard of as far east as the Atlantic coast and as far west as Colorado.

After four years of this work, Mrs. Barry married and retired. There was no one to take her place, yet this period of intense effort had left its mark and its results are not to be undervalued. In any case the Knights of Labor had done their work, had made their contribution and were now to give place to the rising American Federation of Labor, with a platform less vague and all embracing, with a much more definite policy regarding trade organization and better fitted to the needs of the time.

The American Federation of Labor was from the first and is still a federation of national trade unions. These national trade unions decide on their own form of organization and conditions of membership and are represented at conventions by delegates in proportion to their membership. At conventions also are seated representatives from State Federations of Labor and city central labor bodies. The membership of the earliest unions affiliated was overwhelmingly composed of men. The first woman who was heard in the Federation was Mrs. Charlotte Smith. Of her we know that she was in 1882 the President, as she had almost certainly been the founder, of a young organization, termed the Woman's National Industrial League, with headquarters in Washington, Harriet L. Dolsen being the Secretary. It again was one of these hopeful undertakings, begun on a consistent and intelligible theory; assuming that labor conditions for women workers were most degrading, that the woman worker was the most exploited figure in the field of modern industry, and that through co-operative and united effort of the women themselves, of organized labor men, and of socially minded women outside the wage-earning classes, these evils were to be met and overcome. Except that the international note had not been sounded, because the pressing need for it had not as yet arisen, the program reads as if it had been written yesterday. It advocated education for trades and professions; freedom to enter any occupation, equal wages for equal work, equality in the public service (Charlotte Smith lived in Washington), co-operation with all labor associations in standardizing hours of labor. The organization planned to establish branches in all industrial centers.

Mrs. Smith represented the League at the Convention of the Federation of Organized Trades and Labor Unions (the original title of the American Federation of Labor), handing in a memorial asking for advice, assistance and co-operation. She spoke on behalf of the 2,647,157 women wage-earners recorded in the census of 1880. Three years later Mrs. Smith came back. This time she was seated, although without a vote. She was able to secure the passage of a resolution urging the need of the trade union organization of women.

Here and there was found a man who recognized both that the weakness of the woman worker was a handicap to every member of organized labor and also that organized labor owed it to the women themselves to put time, effort and money into the task of bringing them into the labor movement. One of these was the late T. G. Morgan (Tommy Morgan as he was affectionately called to the last). English by birth, and having endured a hard boyhood, he was always pleading the cause of the under dog. During the latter half of his life, when he was no longer working at his trade, he was chiefly known for his activities in connection with the Socialist movement. In 1890, as one of the Chicago delegates to the Convention of the American Federation of Labor, Mr. Morgan introduced and the convention passed a resolution, asking for the submission to Congress of an amendment to the Constitution asking that the vote be given to women. This reform, always advocated by Miss Susan B. Anthony, and under which women vote today, at length became law in 1920.

This same convention of 1890 was notable for the seating of the first fully accredited woman delegate. She was Mrs. Mary Burke, a retail clerk, from Findlay, Ohio. She secured the passing of a resolution recommending the placing in the field of a number of women organizers, to aid in unionizing women workers.

One reason why the woman delegate was at the early conventions of the American Federation so rare a figure is because some of the trades including the largest number of women employes, were then not organized nationally. Of those organizations with women members, the two oldest are the International Typographical Union (1850), and the Cigar Makers' International Union, founded in 1864. All the rest have come into existence since the year 1888; the International Ladies' Garment Workers in 1900, and the United Textile Workers a year later.

In 1891, upon the recommendation of a committee, with

Mrs. Eva McDonald Valesh as Chairman, and Miss Ida Van Etten as Secretary, it was decided to create the office of national organizer, the position to be filled at the beginning of 1892. This was done, and Miss Mary E. Kenney (now Mrs. Mary Kenney O'Sullivan) received the appointment. Mr. Gompers sent Miss Kenney to Boston, where she remained organizing for the Federation for several years, the relationship ending only with her marriage.

The Valesh report had also contained the request that the constitution of the American Federation of Labor be so amended that the woman organizer have a seat on the Executive Board. This, however, was not concurred in.

At the convention of 1894, Mrs. T. J. Morgan ran for the office of first Vice-President, the other candidate being Mr. P. J. McGuire. The result showed 1,865 votes for Mr. McGuire and 226 for Mrs. Morgan, a vote for those days large enough to reflect credit equally upon the woman for whom it was cast and on the men who cast it.

Most of the labor education of women during the closing years of the century was gained through the national unions to which they now were naturally attached. They were included in such different organizations as the Boot and Shoe Workers, Hotel and Restaurant employes and in the United Garment Workers of America, who make men's outer clothing. The United Garment Workers have always made much of the union label upon their products, therefore the men had a distinct motive to encourage them in taking women in. Much more difficult was the unionizing of the makers of women's clothes. It was impossible to stimulate demand for a label among garments as different as a woman's waist, a baby's frock or a ready made dress, with such vast differences in quality, prices and design, and sold to customers few of whom had the faintest idea of what a union label meant or why they should look for it. At that time also the membership of both of these unions was all the time changing its character, for the workers from whom they were yearly recruited were almost entirely foreign, non-English speaking immigrants, whom it was difficult to reach with any message of organization.

The Boot and Shoe Workers' Union was one of the most active and best organized of all the unions with women members. The first few years of its existence were marked by many strikes in which women played their full part. But with the adoption of a union label in 1895 and a new constitution in 1899, the union endorsed the policy to which it for the most part adheres today, of making benefits important, with arbitration clauses and the use of the union label as essential conditions in the agreement with employers.

These examples show that women were at this period beginning to take a place, however humble, in the regular ranks of labor;—humble because they had but little recognition officially and almost no power in directing the policy or administering the affairs of the national union. Whatever experience they gained was in their small locals, and problems were ahead for which that experience offered but inadequate training.

The Working Women's Society of New York aimed principally at the organization of women into trade unions, and also to bring about legislation for their benefit, as well as the efficiency of laws already in existence. It originated in a working women's group. Leonora O'Reilly, a garment worker, whose mother had been a labor woman before her, and who had herself from early days been a member of the Knights of Labor, in 1886 began holding meetings with other workers. Some public-spirited women in New York, with Mrs. Josephine Shaw Lowell at their head, hearing of this effort, asked if they might help, and with their co-operation the Working Women's Society was formed in 1886. The society gave backing and help of all sorts to the feather workers in their strike. It was active also in pushing legislation for the appointment of women factory inspectors. In 1890 success was attained in this respect. An indirect result of this was legislation in Great Britain on the same lines.

The society also undertook the education of the public. Out of its campaigns grew the Consumers' League of New York, which proved to be the beginning of the National Consumers' League, which is still educating the public, the public of a new generation, and steadily pressing forward for improved standards, through legislation.

Chapter IV

WOMEN IN SOME MODERN TRADE UNIONS

In the returns of the national census taken in 1920, women are recorded as being employed in the various occupations and occupational groups.

	Number	Per cent Distribution
All occupations	8,549,399	100.0
Agriculture, forestry and animal husbandry	1,084,074	12.7
Extraction of minerals	3,497	(*)
Manufacturing and mechanical industries	1,931,064	22.6
Transportation	214,262	2.5
Trade	669,919	7.8
Public service (not elsewhere classified)	22,404	0.3
Professional service	1,016,307	11.9
Domestic and personal service	2,184,214	25.6
Clerical occupations	1,423,658	16.7

* Less than one-tenth of one per cent.

So much we know and the Bureau of the Census, in its detailed report gives analysis of how women are distributed among all the subdivisions of the industries. But in striving to discover what number of women are in labor organizations, we find ourselves all at sea. Yet, one of the first questions asked by foreign students or by anyone who is beginning to be interested in the women's labor movement is invariably "How many women trade unionists are there in the United States?" The amazed questioner is told that no one knows.

The Bureau of Labor Statistics has no complete figures,

although some state bureaus have collected information as to their own states. The American Federation of Labor being appealed to, say the officers have no means of measuring the unknown quantity. International unions when asked to supply the numbers of women in their organizations, are often unable to secure it themselves from their locals.

If neither the International Unions nor the A. F. of L. can meet the query, and it is a reasonable one, then it is surely time for some branch of the Department of Labor or for the Bureau of the Census to make an enquiry and supply statistics which are absolutely necessary as a basis for studying and understanding the place which women fill in industry.

For this and other reasons, therefore, the information which follows regarding the status of the different unions with women members, the strength of their woman membership and their activities, is necessarily fragmentary and incomplete; with some of the largest unions it is the more difficult to give a consistent and intelligent picture because the last few years have seen such unusual variations in the standing of the unions themselves.

During the war the labor movement gained greatly both in numerical strength and in power to enforce its claims. After 1920 trade unions suffered in many ways. Cuts in wages were very common; broken time and scarcity of work often caused a great diminution of membership. Further, the unemployment that may have been partly a reaction from the abnormal national expenditure during the war and of the subsequent disorganization of the foreign trade was aggravated by a persistent open shop or anti-union drive on the part of a certain class of employers and corporations.

Under these circumstances, and until fairly accurate

figures have been collected over a term of years, memberships quoted as existing at the particular time are apt to be rather uncertain, the lapse of a few months marring their accuracy even when they have been most carefully collected.

BAKERY AND CONFECTIONERY WORKERS

The Bakery and Confectionery Workers' International Union of America report that at least 75 per cent of the candy workers are women who are hardly organized at all. This is the more serious as it is both a poorly paid trade, and one which is constantly growing in size and importance, coincidently with the war and with the introduction of prohibition. Being a food trade, the sanitary conditions under which the product is made are of the first importance to the public; whereas in the small shops, known as candy kitchens, these are frequently of low standard.

INTERNATIONAL BROTHERHOOD OF BOOKBINDERS

Bookbinding as an occupation is a part of the printing trade, and locals of bookbinders belong to the allied printing trades' council of a city. It is a frequent complaint, nevertheless, that some shops in which the printers are organized, either employ in the bookbinding operations girls who are not organized, or, what is the same thing, have their binding done elsewhere by non-union girls. This is a serious drawback and makes the organization of bindery women somewhat more difficult.

The International Brotherhood of Bookbinders have 175 local unions, 11 of which are composed entirely of women; 110 are made up of both men and women, and the remaining 54 are composed entirely of men. Membership figures recently made up showed 6000 to be women.

In organized shops the members enjoy shorter hours, higher wages and better working conditions all around than obtain in the unorganized shops. The women members seldom act as shop stewards, but hold responsible offices as members of their local. Three out of the eleven executive council members are women and they also do organizing work when the occasion requires. Some of the larger women's locals employ permanent salaried organizers or business agents.

BOOT AND SHOE WORKERS

The average membership of the Boot and Shoe Workers' Union, of whom about one-third are women, is 60,000. The largest organization of women workers is the Stitchers' Local 154 of Brockton, Massachusetts, with a membership of 2909, of whom 95 per cent are women.

The 48 hour week was generally established in the union in the year 1917, although many factories had enjoyed the 48 hour week previously. In 1899 the Boot and Shoe Workers' Union decided to raise their dues to 25 cents a week; of this two-thirds is forwarded to headquarters to cover the general expenses of the union. From the national funds come $5 a week sick benefit, a strike benefit, and disability and death benefit. There are no national agreements, but each locality negotiates with the manufacturers subject to the approval of the national. One board member is always a woman, and one or more women national organizers are employed.

INTERNATIONAL UNION OF UNITED BREWERY, FLOUR, CEREAL AND SOFT DRINKS WORKERS

In a trade which has been so severely hit, and so largely disorganized by prohibition, the employment of women

WOMEN IN MODERN TRADE UNIONS 61

in the bottling departments has greatly decreased. Union membership has suffered in like measure. The women members are now in two or three local unions. Women bottlers benefited greatly through organization. In many instances their wages went up till they were doubled and more than doubled; their hours were reduced to the eight hour day and the 48 hour week. The physical conditions under which they worked were also much improved; the floors were kept dry; there were fewer injuries from broken glass; proper sanitary provision was made and foremen were less overbearing.

Women members have the same position as to dues and benefits as the men. Women members act as secretaries of their unions and as delegates to city central labor bodies.

GLASS BOTTLE BLOWERS

There are scattering members, but they do not make bottles or handle glass; they are packers and do other work around the plants. The officers, although they have had but little success so far with the women, who do not seem to "stay put," hope to get better results in the future.

UNITED CLOTH HAT AND CAPMAKERS OF NORTH AMERICA

This organization, dating from 1901, now claims to be in complete control of the cloth cap and hat making trades, and over a substantial part of the machine made millinery trade.

The makers of caps have long gone through every phase of sweat-shop misery, and from 1902 on the new international maintained an incessant struggle to better conditions. The strikes and the lockouts continued over a series of years. Now there is the week-work system, the 44-hour week, with provision for extra payment for a limited amount of overtime, none of which must fall on Saturdays or holidays.

Women's wages, which had been as low as $8, now range from $25 to $60. The women have also gained a greater dignity and a deeper consciousness.

The membership is at present much below the average, only about 7,000, with 2,000 women members. There are 41 locals in 25 cities. Almost all have women, some women alone. There are women members on a number of local boards, also on the New York local council. There is a national woman organizer.

Owing to the crisis in the trade many quite loyal members of the union are not in financial standing; otherwise the membership would read: total 12,000; women 4,000.

The organization publishes two journals, one in English, the other in Yiddish. Systematic educational work is carried on.

RAILWAY CARMEN.

Of late years women, both white and colored, have become cleaners of the railway coaches. As such they are eligible to membership in the union, but having for the last year been taken into the same lodges, the officials have no record of how many there are. Coach cleaners, whether men or women, rank financially below the mechanics, having lower wages, and paying lower dues, 50 cents a month as against 75 cents for mechanics, and 60 cents for helpers and apprentices. Benefits are paid to all alike, irrespective of amount of dues.

Many women who went in during the war left at its close, often withdrawing in order to give the returning soldier his job again. The women in this employment went out on strike along with the men in the railway

WOMEN IN MODERN TRADE UNIONS 63

shopmen's strike of 1922-1923. In consequence of its long duration, many drifted into other employment.

At the Toronto Convention in August 1921, every woman's lodge sent a delegate with full voting powers. The women delegates took a prominent part in the Convention.

RAILWAY AND STEAMSHIP CLERKS

Through membership in the brotherhood women have been able to secure the same rate of pay when doing the same class of work. There are quite a number of instances of women officers in the local lodges, and a few women have also held positions on the System Board. At times the Grand Lodge has employed women organizers.

Women are found in 765 locals of this organization, and they number between 16,000 and 17,000.

All agreements provide that the pay of women employes shall be the same as that of men for the same class of work, and that working conditions shall be healthful and fitted to their needs. The laws enacted for the government of their employment must be observed.

CIGAR MAKERS' INTERNATIONAL UNION

Cigar making has long been a highly skilled craft, with both men and women employed. Of recent years, however, there has been an increasing use of mechanical appliances, with specializing and team work. This has led to the engaging of unskilled labor, much of it women's labor. The latest figures for the trade, as furnished to the convention of 1920 showed about 50,000 men and 61,000 women, a decrease in seven years of about 15,000 men, as against an increase of about 19,000 women. Of the men, over 33,000 were in the union; of the women, only 7,000. At that convention there was shown an emphatic desire to meet changing conditions by extending jurisdiction over the less skilled, thus inducing women to enter the union. There are many separate locals of women, strippers and banders, besides the women admitted to mixed locals. It is in the separate locals that women show the greatest activity. The improvements the trade union has brought are higher wages, shorter hours, and excellent sanitary standards. It has literally given life to its members. Principally as the result of organization, the death rate among cigar makers from tuberculosis has in twenty years gone down from 51 per cent to 19 per cent. The average age at death, on the other hand, from all causes has increased from 37 to 57 years.

INTERNATIONAL BROTHERHOOD OF ELECTRICAL WORKERS

Besides the telephone operators, dealt with elsewhere, there have been a large number of the women engaged in making electrical supplies and equipment in the men's locals, particularly in Schenectady. Of late years, the women in the movement are not many, except in a few places, such as Chicago, which has still over two hundred members, in a women's local. The effect everywhere upon wages and hours has been very marked. The girls report also decided improvement in the foremen's way of giving orders and in dealing with mistakes or difficulties.

INTERNATIONAL FUR WORKERS' UNION

The fur workers, in their total membership, have about 2,500 women, distributed among eighteen locals. The results of organization have been shorter hours, better wages and much cleaner workshops. From time to time women have taken an active part in the business of their locals as officers and board members.

INTERNATIONAL LADIES' GARMENT WORKERS

The International Ladies' Garment Workers have 90 locals with a membership of over 100,000, of whom about 50 per cent are women workers. All the locals are mixed, including both men and women; even in those locals the bulk of whose membership are women there are men members who work as cutters and pressers since there are no women doing that work. It must be ranked as an industry in which women have made immense advance in wages, hours, and sanitary conditions, all of which advantages they have gained hand in hand with the men. The disappearance of the sweatshop benefited both sexes, the decrease in working hours from 70 or over to 44 has been won through the struggle of both men and women in the industry and both have benefited equally.

The Executive Board of the International has on it one woman vice-president. There are women organizers at work throughout the eastern states. At the last convention there were a number of women delegates in attendance. Women hold many positions as members of local executive boards, local secretaries and managers.

The activities of the women of Locals 22 and 25, the Waist and Dress Makers, in New York, the courage and energy with which they have taken part in all union activities, as well as in pioneering in the field of workers' education, have made of them a shining example to women unionists everywhere.

THE UNITED GARMENT WORKERS

The organization was the original international union controlling makers of men's clothing and affiliated with the American Federation of Labor. It was an organization which always depended largely upon the use of the union label. Men were in the majority. It grew in numbers greatly after the New York strike of 1913 but after the secession of the radical wing at the Nashville Convention of 1914, which ended in the founding of the Amalgamated Clothing Workers, it lost its hold upon many branches of the trade, and in the large cities is now mainly limited to the overalls trade, of which it claims monopoly. They have women organizers.

INTERNATIONAL GLOVE WORKERS OF AMERICA

The glove trade has three divisions, fine kid dress gloves, heavy leather gloves and fabric gloves, the latter including silk, cotton, canton flannel and canvas. Owing to the comparative stiffness of most of the materials used, and the small pieces from which a glove is built up, unusual skill and longer experience than is necessary in most machine sewing processes are required in the operator. The international was chartered in Washington in 1902.

Glove making is one of the subsidiary trades, and therefore it is natural that the organization should not have a very numerous membership. Among its members, however, the proportion of women has always been very high. The standard of the union work accomplished much in abolishing payment for power or machine rent, needles and oil, and in making thoroughly sound ,agreements, agreements which stood the test of eighteen years, renewed, strengthened from time to time, but unbroken during the experience of all those years. It is interesting also because it has always been largely officered by women. It was one of the first unions to feel the effect of the open shop drive in the fall of 1920. The five-months' strike which followed in Chicago has seriously crippled it everywhere. One by-result of the strike was the opening of a small co-operative glove factory. Gloves are usually thought of as luxuries, yet the greater proportion of the gloves made in this country are worn by teamsters, street car men, railroad men, farmers and electricians. With the exception of the farmers, all the others are in organized trades, are keenly interested in encouraging union labor, and prefer to wear union-made gloves. The railroad men especially supported the project from the start.

HOTEL AND RESTAURANT EMPLOYES

In no trade have more miserable conditions existed than among the waitresses before the days of organization. In none are the results of co-operative effort more clearly to be seen. There are 186 locals with women members. Sometimes the local will have none but women and it is then a waitresses' local. More often the locals are mixed. In either case, all form part of Hotel and Restaurant Employees' International Alliance.

In the majority of union establishments gone are the old abuses, such as having to do "side work," including among other tasks the mopping of dining-room floors, washing chairs and tables, washing and ironing of napkins, and the preparing of vegetables. Union waitresses also have their own separate toilet and rest rooms, with individual clothing lockers and ready laundered aprons. They are protected against the many insults and liberties that a young girl standing alone has to meet. They can expect a wage of from $15 to $18 a week, with two proper meals. They have one day a week off, and an eight hour day, which must not extend over nine hours. Many women are local officers, and the general Secretary-Treasurer describes them, after they have overcome their first feeling of timidity and inexperience, as active and loyal, and "gluttons for work." There is one woman board member, and there have been women employed for years as national organizers.

Waitresses are a wandering race. They carry their trade along with them, knowing that everywhere people have to eat. Wherever they go, they make new friends, so there is more exchanging of ideas between girls, between organized and unorganized, than in many other occupations. This has resulted in many non-union places agreeing to live up to something like union standards. The employers have yielded to the demands of even unorganized girls, fearing that if they refused their employes might join the union.

LAUNDRY WORKERS INTERNATIONAL UNION

The Laundry Workers have 92 local unions, all of them with women members in the proportion of about 80 per cent of the whole, about 4,000. Almost all union laundries work the eight hour day and they give a minimum wage of not less than $15 a week. Unorganized women laundry workers often work nine hours, and in some southern states, ten hours, with a wage averaging from $9 to $10 a week. This poor showing is particularly common in the southern states. The union also guarantees higher sanitary standards, such as having women's dressing rooms separate from the dressing rooms of the male employes.

Women members occupy most of the offices in the local unions. In the large San Francisco local, with 1,800 members, the offices are divided up. President, a man; vice-president, a woman; secretary and assistant secretary, women; business agent, a man. The general executive

WOMEN IN MODERN TRADE UNIONS

board has nine members of whom one is a woman; she and occasionally others, do organizing.*

UNITED LEATHER WORKERS

There are many women engaged in the leather industry, unorganized. The international union is doing everything within its power to bring them into the labor movement, so that they may enjoy the benefits of united action.

AMALGAMATED MEAT CUTTERS AND BUTCHER WORKMEN OF NORTH AMERICA

The story of the organization of the girls in the meat-packing plants of Chicago and other large cities is a discouraging one. Twice there have been large groups organized in Chicago; in 1902 when the larger proportion of the workers were Irish and American in nationality, and again in 1920-1921, with a membership chiefly Polish, but also embracing other nationalities. On both occasions there has been a long maintained struggle for better industrial standards, and on both occasions the struggle has been lost by the workers. While the organization still remains, it now includes no women.

NATIONAL FEDERATION OF POST OFFICE CLERKS

Women take an important share in the safe and speedy transportation and distribution of our mail; there being no fewer than 590 locals with women, accounting for a total

---

*For an account of what organization has done in laundries the reader should consult "Women in Trade Unions in San Francisco." Lillian R. Matthews. University of California, 1913. Miss Matthews' account of laundry conditions is summarized in the "Trade Union Woman." Alice Henry.

of 4,000 women members. The second vice-president is a woman, who is active in organization work in the Western States District. Many locals have voluntary women organizers, but none paid.

RAILROAD TELEGRAPHERS

The Order of Railroad Telegraphers have about 3,000 women in their union. Dues and benefits are the same. From time to time they have employed a woman organizer.

There are 144 subordinate divisions, practically all of which have women members. Wages have been increased 200 per cent since organizing, hours of labor reduced from an unlimited number to eight per day and the working month reduced from 31 to 26 days. Women are eligible to any office in the organization, and invariably take an active part in the affairs of the subordinate divisions.

INTERNATIONAL TYPOGRAPHICAL UNION

There are over 2,000 union women printers, which is but a fraction of the whole organization, totaling about 75,000. The women are distributed among the locals, between eight and nine hundred in number. A woman sometimes serves as secretary of a local, and Miss Anna Wilson, of Washington, was for several years a member of the Board of Trustees of the Union Printers' Home at Colorado Springs. There are usually one or more women delegates at the conventions, and women are serving their respective local unions in various capacities in all sections of the country.

UPHOLSTERERS' INTERNATIONAL UNION

The Upholsterers' International Union, with a total membership of over 8,000, has over 2,000 women members, and five locals composed of women exclusively. Six locals are mixed. Women organizers are occasionally employed by the International, and there are women organizers in locals in several large cities. This organization stands out in the labor movement of America, in that the constitution makes it compulsory to have at least two women on the Executive Board. The results of organization have been increase of wages, shortening of hours and improvement of working conditions.

UNIONS UNAFFILIATED WITH THE AMERICAN FEDERATION OF LABOR

The organizations touched upon so far have all been unions affiliated with the American Federation of Labor. There are also national labor unions with women, which for one reason or another are not in such affiliation, but which nevertheless cannot be overlooked, the most important being the Amalgamated Clothing Workers of America. Besides national groupings there are, particularly in the East, many independent local unions with women who draw their membership from one city or district only. Most of them are in the textile and the shoe industries.

AMALGAMATED CLOTHING WORKERS OF AMERICA

Among the unaffiliated groups this is the largest organization containing women. As a separate body it dates back to the Nashville Convention of the United Garment Workers of 1914 when most of the locals, composed of the Slavic-Jewish and other foreign workers, seceded, and formed the new union.

The most recent figures to hand give a membership of 140,000, of whom about 57,400 are women. The larger number of these are employed in Chicago and Rochester, New York; Baltimore and Boston come next.

There are 148 locals, all of them containing women members, except one or two cutters' locals and the pressers' locals. Seven of the joint boards in the large cities have women secretaries. The secretarial work for 33 locals out of the entire 148 is done by women. There have also been many women organizers, both Jewesses and Gentiles, maintained from headquarters.

TEXTILE UNIONS

In April, 1919, great textile strikes were in progress in Lawrence, Massachusetts, and in Paterson and Passaic, New Jersey, and other textile centers. Thus it came about that groups of workers either not belonging to the United Textile Workers or desiring to secede from them, met in New York in April, 1919, along with knit goods workers, and the Amalgamated Textile Workers of America was formed. About one-third of the membership is women, divided among silk workers in New York City, and woolen workers in the southern New England States. There is no separate report of work done but they make an excellent showing in regular organization work.

The American Federation of Textile Operatives is a secession organization, which broke away from the United Textile Workers on questions of payment of dues and per capita tax. Although a national organization, it is reported as waning. Its influence is mainly in New England, the largest locals being in and around Fall River, New Bedford and Salem.

WOMEN IN MODERN TRADE UNIONS

SHOE WORKERS' UNIONS

The shoe industry is one of those in which there exist cross currents of independent organization. During the last thirty years there have been several secessions from the Boot and Shoe Workers' Union. The best known of these seceding groups or dual organizations is the United Shoe Workers of America. In Lynn there is a very large local of Lady Stitchers.

INDUSTRIAL WORKERS OF THE WORLD

The Industrial Workers of the World hold any woman who works for wages eligible to membership, and they report a large number of women members. Although it is impossible to supply details, there are women members in the textile groups and also large numbers among the fruit pickers, canners and other seasonal migratory workers on the Pacific Coast; also educational workers and foodstuffs workers. Women speak and act as delegates.

SOME TYPICAL SITUATIONS: SHIRTS AND COLLARS

The shirt and collar industry is one of those concentrated almost entirely in one district, in and around the city of Troy, N. Y. We cannot help knowing this if it were from nothing but the advertisements of good looking young men displaying the very latest fashion in collars as they meet our eyes on railway platforms and in street cars. Ninety per cent of all the shirts and collars used in this country are said to be made in that one spot.

Troy is also a laundry center, as the shirt and collar factories run their own huge laundries. The laundrying of the collar is quite as important as the cutting or the sewing.

The name of Troy is associated with two huge strikes in the laundry branch of the trade. The first of these strikes was in 1869. There was a most active and prosperous union in existence. The organization had raised the wages of its members from an average of two or three dollars a week to a scale of from eight to fourteen dollars, according to the class of work.

Under Kate Mullaney, who the year before had been made national organizer of women for the National Labor Union, the workers went on strike for a raise. After a long hard struggle they were beaten and the union crushed.

The lifetime of a whole generation passed away and succession after succession of workers filled the Troy factories, when in 1905 the workers of that day were faced with their own troubles. The employes, 22,000 in number, of whom 8,000 were women, were almost entirely American born. The Manufacturers' Association included eight firms working under a rigid agreement. During the preceding few years a change had taken place in the management of the industry. The older women described how they had enjoyed short hours, eight hours being quite common, not going to work until nine o'clock. Speaking and laughing formerly allowed were now heavily fined. There was great strictness regarding punctuality, three days' fine, for instance, for being three minutes late on account of ice. Work was irregular, some girls being kept on all day but given work only for an hour or two. There would be a 20 or 25 cents fine for dropping a collar on the floor and the fine even reached to a dollar if collars became soiled on the drying bars.

Eleven girls asked to see the manager but were put off and refused. They were afterwards summarily dismissed, in a manner which deeply offended them.

The principal grievance was the introduction of the

WOMEN IN MODERN TRADE UNIONS

starching machine. It was scalding hot work using the machine. The first machine introduced cut the prices from four to two cents a dozen. The regular workers were laid off and new raw help taken in.

The girls chose their leader, Bernard Feldman, but they largely directed the strike themselves. It was the first of a new kind of strike among women. The girls raised $25,000, visiting other cities for the purpose. They drew financial aid from the International Laundry Workers' Union but before the strike ended there were serious disputes between the local and the international. Meanwhile the laundry workers made bold demands upon the sympathies of the citizens and especially of other women.

Mrs. Rheta Childe Dorr was then Chairman of the Industrial Committee of the General Federation of Women's Clubs, and she wrote and spoke for them. Miss Mary Terry, the local president, and Mrs. Dora Brophy appealed for help to Miss Gertrude Barnum, national organizer for the newly organized New York Women's Trade Union League, and she and others, including Miss Ida Rauh, Miss Martha Bensley (Mrs. Robert Bruere), and Miss Stokes, represented the Women's Trade Union League most effectively.

The women of the League tried to effect a settlement in which they were supported by the Mayor of the city and the Troy Federation of Labor. The New York State Department of Labor report for 1905 states quite clearly that it was the employers who steadily refused arbitration, although the workers desired it and asked for it.

As the months went on funds became exhausted, courage sapped and the girls found it impossible to hold out.

This strike too, like the earlier one, ended in seeming defeat, but called attention to many evils which were remedied, made for better conditions for laundry workers, and helped to educate the public to a sense of responsibility for industrial unrest, and was of nation-wide significance in calling attention to the possibility of arbitration in industrial disputes.

THE TEXTILE INDUSTRY

The textile industry, which employs vast numbers of women, differs greatly from garment making; the latter is a trade requiring little capital and the workers have continually to face the menace of new small shops springing up that have to be brought into line. Textile mills do not spring up over night like this as they require large sums of capital before a start can be made, but on the other hand the capital is far more strongly entrenched and employers more closely linked together. The textile industry covers woven, knitted or felted goods, from carpets to lace, and made of wool, silk, or any kind of fibre; goods in the piece or made-up articles, like sweaters or stockings.

The textile industry has a great hold upon New England and North Atlantic states. Fall River and Lowell are still as they were one hundred years ago, great mill centers. Further south, Paterson, New Jersey, and Philadelphia are other localities dotted with silk mills. The latter is the largest single textile center in the country. Innumerable other towns in Pennsylvania are given over to the same trade. The processes, especially of preparation and finishing, are somewhat different in the woolen, cotton and silk plants. The South Atlantic states are extensive producers of cotton yarn.

The vastness of the trade is thus described in the American Labor Year Book for 1921:

In the value of its annual product and of capitalization, the textile industry ranks second and third, respectively, among the leading industries of the United States. In number of workers it stands first, running well over a million in all its branches. Most people in thinking of textile processes, think only of weavers, spinners and loomfixers. In a worsted mill of common type, there are often as many as 25 separate jobs or occupations.

Some of these jobs are highly skilled, requiring long training, and where there are effective unions, several years of apprenticeship. Others require little training or skill. Still others are machine tending occupations which can be filled by an immigrant who has never seen the inside of a factory, or by a ten year old child.

A SHOE WORKERS' STRIKE

The efficiency and careful management of the long established and conservative Boot and Shoe Workers' Union was recently severely tested. The Boot and Shoe Manufacturers' Association, Cincinnati, in 1922 unsuccessfully proposed to their operatives a reduction of wages of from ten to twenty-five per cent. A second proposal of ten per cent met with no better fate. The national officers tried to effect a settlement, but in vain; and at length, although unwillingly, sanctioned the calling of a strike. There was a great deal of unemployment at the time. For seven months 3,000 workers remained out, of whom fewer than 100 returned to work.

Representatives of the government on two occasions endeavored to effect a compromise.

One remarkable feature was the national handling of the situation. The officers had certainly not desired a strike; but they realized that the maintenance of the entire organization was at stake, and that if beaten in Cincinnati, the same process would have to be gone through in every large shoe center. The recognition of the union and the re-employment of strikers were the two points on which they could not afford to be beaten. Sanctioning the strike meant the undertaking to pay strike benefit as long as the struggle should last. This was accordingly done. Twice, however, not being desirous of lowering their benefit balance below the amount that should be maintained as a guarantee to members of the payment of sick, death and disability benefits, and being unwilling to make an assessment, the General Executive Board appealed to the entire membership for contributions to the Cincinnati strike fund. Results justified this course, for the sum thus raised, supplemented by donations from general funds of the organization enabled the National Executive Board to pay out to every striker the full constitutional strike benefit, up till the time that the strike was called off.

The settlement provided for the acceptance of a reduction of five per cent on piece work and day hands, with an additional five per cent on 36 pair lots; the reduction not to apply to any day workers earning less than $14.00 a week. The union was recognized and relations between union committees and manufacturers' committees and representatives were renewed.

THE NEEDLE TRADES

The needle trades cover the industry employing women which has accomplished most during the last twenty years, although the effect of what they have done has only become visible since 1910. Of the organizations included the largest are the Amalgamated Clothing Workers of America (unaffiliated with the A. F. of L.), the United Garment Workers and the International Ladies' Garment Workers, in regular affiliation. Besides these there are the United Cloth Hat and Cap Makers and Fur Workers.

Shoe Workers and Glove Workers, although their trades

WOMEN IN MODERN TRADE UNIONS 79

are essentially sewing crafts, are always thought of in connection with the leather trades, from the material of which most of their product is composed.

The workers in all of these occupations are almost entirely immigrants from Eastern Europe, and mostly Slavic Jews, with Poles, Bohemians, Hungarians, Lithuanians and Italians. In the International Ladies' Garment Workers the Cloakmakers were the pioneers. They took the first steps towards forming an international of all those making women's garments. The trade was then a sweated trade carried on in the sweatshops and the tenements of the large cities. With the beginnings of organization opposition to the claims for union terms and for improved conditions was redoubled. In 1905 the Reefer Makers declared a strike, pressing the point that they should not have to find their own machines. The strike was one of the most hotly contested, accompanied by even more than the usual violence, slugging of the unionists, needless arrests and jail sentences. But the workers won. The Shirt Waist Makers were the next group to rise. Almost simultaneously in New York, Boston, and Philadelphia the unorganized workers went out—in New York alone, to the number of 40,000. This industrial uprising began in November, 1909, and lasted until February, 1910. The women were to the front everywhere. It was a girls' strike, and the partial victory won was a girls' victory. The result was largely brought about through the support of the New York Women's Trade Union League.

The actual terms of settlement, and the actual numbers enrolled in the union mattered less than did the example they had set to all other needle-workers. Even girls could win; even Jewesses, individualists as they were, could be organized, and being organized, could show the road to be followed. The general strike (moved by Clara

Lemlich, at the meeting in Cooper Union, where Mr. Gompers presided, when with hand upraised, she called upon her fellows to keep the old Jewish oath of faith to one another) had taught them something. Such a strike could so tie up an unorganized industry that, given patience and endurance, manufacturers would come to terms and recognize the union.

The strikes of the shirt-waist girls stirred the workers in the cloak industry. If the girls could achieve notable gains by a fight to a finish, then surely it was a shame for the cloakmakers much longer to submit to the semi-slavery which then prevailed in the shops. This resulted in the calling of a general strike of the cloakmakers in New York City in June, 1910. After seven weeks the protocol was signed by the Cloak Manufacturers' Association and the union. Relations were established upon a union basis with a Board of Grievances and a Board of Arbitration. "The Protocol," writes one member, "with the association of influential manufacturers practically substituted mediation, arbitration and the collective bargain for the shop strikes that had been so habitual with the work people in the past."

In 1913, the International Ladies' Garment Workers' Union started an energetic organization campaign among its women workers, and made preparations for general strikes of the Waist and Dress Makers, the White Goods Workers, the Wrapper and Kimono Workers, and the Children's Dressmakers.

The Waist and Dress Manufacturers of New York City, remembering the heroic struggle of the Shirt Waist Makers in 1909, their bravery and self-sacrifice, and remembering also their own money losses, and anxious to avoid a repetition of that struggle, entered into negotiations with the General Executive Board of the International Ladies' Garment Workers' Union and agreed to a collective agreement similar in all respects to the protocol of the cloak industry. This occurred in June, 1913. Since then they have had to wage hard struggles for their organizations several times, but the Waist and Dressmakers' Union is a reality today and a factor not only in the International Ladies' Garment Workers, but in the labor movement as a whole. They were the first to struggle for the 44-hour week, in 1919, and also for the 40-hour, 5-day week in the needle industry, which they won in February, 1923.

The International Ladies' Garment Workers in 1914 at their convention appropriated $1,500 for educational activities, and classes were organized in the Rand School. In 1915 the Waistmakers Local 25 organized its own classes in a public school building under the name of Unity Center, in co-operation with the New York Board of Education. At the following convention the plan of the Waistmakers was accepted and more Unity Centers were opened, with Miss Juliet Stuart Poyntz as director and Miss Fannia M. Cohn as executive secretary, who is still continuing in that capacity.

What the girls tried out the International has developed to a remarkable degree.

At present the International Ladies' Garment Workers' Union appropriates $17,500 a year for the education of its members. The educational department, through which extensive educational work is carried on, includes activities for almost every group of its large membership. These are free to all union members.

In New York there are now eight Unity Centers. Since most of the members are of foreign birth, English is taught in all of the Centers. In addition to the English classes, the union independently arranges courses in applied economics, history and problems of the labor movement, and the development of industry. They also have classes in physical training under trained teachers. The international also has a Workers' University, where courses in the social sciences, literature and psychology are given, arranged for the more advanced members. The classes meet on Saturday afternoons and Sunday mornings.

In 1920, seven locals of the I. L. G. W. U. established their own Union Health Center for all the members of the International Ladies' Garment Workers' Union. This includes a medical service and a dental clinic with special lectures and courses on health subjects. The union provided and equipped one of the most modern health centers of its kind. This is the first time that a union has carried on its own health service for its own members. The center is a self-supporting, cooperative institution, with emphasis upon preventive medicine and industrial hygiene, taking for its motto, "In sanitation and in health as well as wealth, the salvation of the workers depends on the working class itself."

The Joint Board of Sanitary Control in New York which has upon it representatives of the employers, the union and the public, keeps a constant oversight on fire hazards, right posture and seating, toilet facilities, light, ventilation and heating.

The general strike among the makers of men's clothing which struck Chicago in the Fall of 1910, included at first, few trade unionists. The workers poured out of the unorganized shops till in a brief time 50,000 were supposed to be out. This lasted five months. In addition to looking to the local and national union of the The United Garment Workers, the strikers had the strong backing of the Chicago Federation of Labor and the Chicago Women's Trade Union League. Besides putting the garment workers' case before the public, providing bail, and protecting both girls and men, these organizations established commissary stores which made the strikers' money go much farther, and enabled them to hold out long.

The most notable result of the strike was the return to work under an agreement of the thousands of employes of Hart, Schaffner and Marx. It was a signed agreement, which permitted no discrimination against strikers. It has stood the test of time, the administrative machinery being gradually developed, and its terms agreed to by other manufacturers, until now all the large manufacturing centers have the plants organized upon this system. When the Amalgamated Clothing Workers was formed as an independent organization, relations with the employer firms were maintained.

In some of the large cities, the women's energies have found scope through the general women's local, which they have themselves established. The women may transfer from the ordinary mixed local, such as a pants makers, or a coat makers, and take out a card in the women's local. In Chicago, for example, there are 600 girls so organized, with Anna Snyder as president, who conduct their own affairs under their own officers. They are represented on the Joint Board by five delegates. The president of the Board of Directors of the Joint Board itself is a woman, Clara Leon.

The women's local co-operates, not only on the economic side of the industrial struggle, but in the educative activities, in managing the symphony concerts and lectures, and in class work. They are planning to have a swimming pool and a gymnasium in the new headquarters.

In Rochester, N. Y., a similar women's local has 6,000 members, a large proportion active. The women furnish their quota of shop chairmen, and every shop has its girls' committee. There is an executive committee of ten girls, who plan on speakers and other activities for the local. They also take their part in directing classes and general educational meetings. Sadie Goodman is but a type of the experienced women leaders, whether in strikes, in settlements or in the ordinary every day work. There are seven women delegates to the Joint Board in Rochester. Similar conditions prevail in Baltimore.

The smaller the city, the greater the activity. In Louisville, the business agent and leader of the Clothing Workers is a woman, Emma Saurer. In Minneapolis and St. Paul, the secretary-treasurer of the Twin City Joint Board is Florence Wallin. Milwaukee, again, is another center of energy among the women. Most of these groups are in large degree composed of Americans.

At the National Convention in 1922, over twenty of the delegates were women.

CHAPTER V

WOMEN IN SOME MODERN TRADE UNIONS
(Continued)

Nearly a hundred years have passed since textile workers and shoe workers and sewing workers began to feel their way towards concerted effort as the only way to meet the increasing pressure of modern industry, and among all the trades employing women, spinning and weaving, and making of shoes and the making of clothes are by general consent still well to the front as organized groups, both for the number of women employed and for the number organized. Now women have been drawn into other occupations, into new classes of work whether in factory, shop, office or classroom. Gradually, in spite of social prejudice, thousands of women have been educated up to an understanding of what the collective bargain means for them, and have come into the trade unions of their occupation. We have seen this with bookbinders, tobacco workers and cigar makers, and waitresses and laundresses. The last few years have seen the women in some of the more modern occupations also enrolling themselves in trade unions, sometimes entering those already organized by men, and sometimes forming their own. Such groups are teachers, telephone operators, federal employes and stage performers. In none of these is organization as yet very extensive, but the pioneering spirit is there.

TEACHERS

The first teachers to unionize were the classroom teachers of Chicago, where salaries had failed to keep pace with the rising cost of living, or bear any relation to the increasing demands made upon teachers. Through Margaret Haley and the late Catherine Goggin, the Chicago Teachers' Federation was formed, which then and ever since has embraced a large proportion of the city's grade teachers. As an organization it has experienced varying fortunes. It won its first great victory for increased salaries through the wit and ability of its leaders, who discovered that large amounts of money owing to the city by certain corporate interests were not being collected. Through suit after suit, into court after court, they patiently carried their case; first to see that the money was paid, and next to see that some of it came the teachers' way. The teachers, almost all women, early learned that organized labor was their best friend; also that the teachers of the children and the parents of the children, the latter in great majority working people, had many interests in common. The Federation, therefore, in 1902, on invitation from the Chicago Federation of Labor, affiliated with that body, sending delegates to all meetings.

In 1915 the Board adopted the Loeb rule under which teachers were forbidden to affiliate with labor, and in their right to do this, the Board was sustained by the courts. In the meantime the Board had dropped sixty-eight teachers without warning, and without any charges having been made against them. A large number were Federation teachers and officers. They were women marked "good," "excellent," "superior" and so on.

In order to settle the matter, and remove all excuse for not reinstating them, and to end an impossible situation, Mr. John Fitzpatrick, organizer for the American Federation of Labor and President of the Chicago Federation of Labor, in a report made in 1916 to the latter body formally recommended the withdrawal of the Chicago Teachers' Federation from all its affiliations with organized labor; but he urged the passing of legislation, then pending in the legislature, which should forbid public officials from discriminating against public employes. Had this been passed, the Loeb rule would at once have ceased to exist.

Both the men's and the women's locals of high school teachers remained in affiliation with labor, and have increased their membership.

Meanwhile, and largely through the influence of the Chicago group, there had been formed teachers' locals in many different cities, locals united in a national organization, the American Federation of Teachers. The teachers of the New York schools, and the Washington, D. C., high school teachers were among the earliest to take this step. Teachers' unions exist in Paterson, Buffalo, Atlanta, Memphis, St. Paul, Minneapolis, Sacramento and Portland. They have often been able to obtain increases of salaries, or else maintain salary schedules in face of threatened reduction. It must be realized by most people how extremely low is the remuneration of teachers almost everywhere outside the large cities.

The affiliation with organized labor has frequently enabled organized teachers to carry out their ideals. In this way, they have led in the movement for bringing about such modern improvements as, dividing the children into smaller classes, and saving the cultural part of the school program from being swamped by the advocates of vocational training, and in general, broadening the scope of school work. Teachers begin to realize that whatever improves working conditions for every one, helps directly to improve the educational work done for and by the children. The union movement has strengthened in teachers the sense of our public educational system as a social function of the community, rather than as a group of jobs sustained by a budget, and directed by academic captains.

TELEPHONE OPERATORS

The management of the American Telegraph and Telephone Company sets down certain policies of administration in relation to operators, but in a corporation composed of so many subsidiary companies, it is evident that there must be great differences of practice in different places. Therefore, in speaking of the telephone industry, the writer is making no general criticism of conditions, either in the American Telegraph and Telephone Company, and its subsidiary companies, or in any of the small, independent companies, but is describing the beginnings of unionism among the telephone operators themselves, as these were manifested at the time.

The organization of telephone operators dates back only to 1912, when twenty telephone operators, employed in the toll exchange of Boston came together and talked over the situation. Wages were low, overtime a moot point, but the chief complaint was what is called the "split trick," that is, the spreading of the day's working hours over a long period, stretching a day nominally about eight hours long into one that might easily extend over fourteen hours. The girl might go on duty at seven o'clock in the morning and yet her work might not end until nine o'clock at night. She had time off in the afternoon, when it was of little use to her, as she often traveled backwards and forwards a long distance to her home, and extra carfare might come out of her own pocket. With the aid of Miss Mabel Gillespie, of the Boston Women's Trade Union League, and of the late Mr. Peter F. Linehan, general organizer of the International Brotherhood of Electrical Workers, they formed a sub-local of the Boston linemen's local.

They then took their complaints to the New England Bell Telephone Company. The union claims that the eight and a half hour day was then established, the vacation period extended to two weeks, the use of the split trick greatly lessened and carfare allowed in all cases, and overtime paid time and a half. Before long the eight hour day was in force. Another point the Telephone Operators Department makes is that one of the significant things the union accomplished was to ensure that such measures as did exist for the benefit of the employes under the company's own regulations were enforced.

Under the influence and the wise counsel of Mr. Linehan, the girls learnt the value of restraint and moderation in their negotiations with the company, and recognition was at last achieved. When a twelve dollar a week wage was the main point at issue a strike was very near, the company having girls from a distance housed, some even at the Copley-Plaza, on hand to take the place of the regular operators. The settlement was finally reached between the company and the union at a conference arranged by the Boston Chamber of Commerce, there having been throughout no interruption of service.

New England has been the only part of the country to be thoroughly organized. There are locals, however, in the central states and some in the west.

The girls have gradually risen to a recognized status in the International Brotherhood of Electrical Workers, after the subject had been brought to two regular conventions, and at one special convention in 1918. At first under the constitution of the international, they had to be members of a sub-local, subsidiary to a men's local, and with no power of self-government. Afterwards the telephone operators were formed into a department, with complete self-government and control of their own finances. The Telephone Operators Department is the only women's trade union holding its own national convention.

FEDERAL EMPLOYES

The National Federation of Federal Employes was chartered by the American Federation of Labor in 1917, following a convention of delegates from about 60 locals in various parts of the United States. Local No. 1 of San Francisco is credited as the first, but the actual beginning of what is now the National Federation was the Women's Union in the Bureau of Engraving and Printing which was chartered as Federal Employes' Union No. 12776, by the American Federation of Labor in 1909. This local has now a membership of a little under 2,000 of women engaged upon fifteen different processes in the making, counting, sorting and examining of paper money, stamps, government bonds, certificates, etc., in the Bureau of Engraving and Printing, the only institution of its kind in the United States.

The Federation of Federal Employes was given jurisdiction over all employes of the United States Government except those exclusively eligible to existing national or international unions affiliated with the American Federation of Labor. This excludes the postal service with the exception of the Post Office Department employes in Washington, as distinguished from the City Post Office there, and it also excludes the craft organizations having members in

WOMEN IN MODERN TRADE UNIONS

government service, except as such members desire to carry more than one card.

As federal employes are the servants of the United States, the final resort for them must be Congress, as the agent of the people of the United States. Hence all of their demands must at length come before Congress, and their state can be improved, and injustices righted, chiefly through legislation.

The Federation now has 262 locals, with membership in every state and in all the territorial possessions of the United States.

The active career of the Federation may be said to have begun in 1917 when Representative Borland of Missouri introduced an amendment to an appropriation bill lengthening the government working day without increasing compensation. Up till then government employes in the District of Columbia were supposed to work not less than seven hours a day, but might be asked to work, and in many bureaus they did work, any number of hours overtime, without further remuneration. This bill prescribed the minimum numbers of hours to be worked as eight, with no relief as to the number of extra hours of work that might be put in for the same pay. Mr. Borland based his arguments upon economy of tax payers' money. He and other supporters of the bill tried to win over the sympathy of the trade unionists, saying that the object of the bill was only to obtain for civil servants the same hours as other working men had to put in.

The issue in the public mind was thus extremely confusing. The bill was known popularly but misleadingly as the Civil Service Eight-Hour bill. As an eight-hour law stands in the public mind for something good and desirable, it was incomprehensible that civil servants and the labor leaders supporting them, should be found objecting to an eight-hour day. Opposition was set down to the natural indolence of unenterprising and irresponsible government officials. At this stage the employes in the District of Columbia organized and by distributing information regarding the true meaning of the bill and by arranging hearings, succeeded in defeating it.

Among the women members of the Federation are to be found librarians, nurses, editors, statisticians, investigators in social economics, doctors, biologists, and various others who are usually classified in the professional occupations. The largest group numerically of the women in the organization are clerks, stenographers, typists and those in the industrial establishments, such as the Bureau of Engraving and Printing, mail equipment shop, flag making department of the Navy Yards, etc. There are also a considerable number of women who are in the government institutions as matrons, on the housekeeping staff, and on the teaching staff; and in the prisons there are women who act as guards and supervisors of the prison work.

The late Dr. E. B. Rosa, Physicist of the Bureau of Standards, was once asked "Why should a federal employe join the union?" This was his reply:

The primary purpose of the Federal Employes' Union is to improve conditions in the government service, to raise the standard of the personnel, to increase the efficiency of administration, and to better the average performance of the government workers. Every employe of the government should be in sympathy with these aims, and should be willing to aid by joining the union and doing his part in so worthy a cause. In helping to make the government service more efficient and more attractive to able and ambitious men and women, one is not merely stimulating and helping his fellow employes, but he is rendering a permanent service to the government itself.

ACTORS

An unusual episode in recent labor history was the strike of stage performers of 1919. The organizations involved were the Actors' Equity Association, then in existence about five years, and the Producing Managers' Association, which included a large number of producers. The strike arose out of the affiliation or plans for affiliation of Equity with the American Federation of Labor, and the unwillingness of the managers to continue to recognize the Actors' Association under these changed conditions.

Strikes of garment workers, when on a large scale, are more or less carried on in the public eye, through picketing, police activities, and court prosecutions. A street car strike brings home to the man and woman in the street that an industrial struggle is on. In the one case public interest often fades prematurely, and in the other an inconvenient situation has to be met by the substitution of all kinds of primitive modes of transportation; but to the public an actors' strike for the most part meant a unique entertainment. It might be serious enough to both sides in the dispute, who were equally losing money. A strike initiated by a mass meeting at the Hotel Astor, followed a few days later by the closing of thirteen New York theaters, which remained closed for a whole month, a strike extending from New York to Boston, Chicago and Philadelphia, was something of a novelty. The stars of the profession and even the actor-managers were divided, but many of the most prominent sided with the striking performers. One reason why it was so remarkable was that theatrical people were running it. The publicity organized was of the most dramatic, not to say sensational sort, so that interest was kept alive. One plan in New York, was the giving of performances in the Lexington Opera House, one of the largest metropolitan

94 WOMEN AND THE LABOR MOVEMENT

houses. Besides providing nightly a first class performance with such actresses as Ethel Barrymore in serious parts and Marie Dressler in vaudeville, it was the custom to have a speech or two. The stars gave their services, and it was through such support that the chorus girls were helped to tide over their weeks out of work. Nothing was more remarkable than the intense activity of the entire profession. There was no actor of prominence that was not involved on one side or the other. Samuel Gompers addressed a mass meeting of actors and actresses, pledging them the backing of organized labor. While all this was going on, other large meetings of protest were being held nightly at the Hotel Biltmore. The stars numbered among the directors of the Fidelity League, the rival actors association, were leaders and speakers at these meetings. The end came as suddenly as the beginning. Managers and actors came to terms, and on September 6th an agreement was signed, to run for four years.

Simultaneously the chorus girls formed an organization, which, it is claimed, has brought about many improvements in their lot, notably, that they no longer have to provide the expensive shoes, stockings, hats and wigs necessary to their roles, nor have they to attend an unlimited number of rehearsals without payment.

LOCAL LABOR UNIONS

Where there is no international union in a trade, there are, nevertheless, scattered all over the country, in the large industrial centers, and in small towns, numbers of local unions chartered directly by the A. F. of L. Many of these have women members; several none but women. Among organizations with women members are button workers, court reporters, crab pickers, domestic workers, envelop

WOMEN IN MODERN TRADE UNIONS

makers, feather and flower workers, gold leaf cutters, hair dressers, hair spinners, hat trimmers, hospital nurses and attendants, municipal employes, neckwear workers, office employes, park employes, scientific laboratory workers, suspender workers, theatrical wardrobe attendants, and wire sewers, besides a number of general federal labor unions in small places, which admit wage-earners in different trades into a common group.

WOMEN LABOR LEADERS AND ORGANIZERS

In 1908, Miss Anna Fitzgerald, of the Upholsterers' Union and President of the International Women's Label League was appointed general woman organizer for the American Federation of Labor and served for six months. This action came principally as the result of a request made at interstate conferences of the National Women's Trade Union League, held simultaneously in Boston, New York and Chicago.

From 1908 up to the present, thirty-eight women have acted as organizers under the American Federation of Labor; many of them for short periods, a few weeks or months, to meet an emergency, or a special organizing drive, their services being contributed to one of the international or local unions, to aid in strengthening labor organization in that trade. Miss Mary Kelleher was in the field for over six years; Miss Melinda Scott for four years, while Miss Anna Neary, who began to serve in 1917, was still organizing in 1923. That there was but one general organizer at that time is partly to be accounted for by the period of extreme depression and consequent unemployment under which the labor movement had had to struggle. One of the most unfortunate consequences of long continued unemployment is the loss of membership that follows, through absolute inability to pay dues. The local union is the first to feel the effects; next the international, and finally the American Federation of Labor itself. Under these circumstances, every organization had been compelled to economize and cut down its staff of organizers, and it is therefore not remarkable that women, who had been the latest officers to be engaged, were often the first whose services were dispensed with. Of recent years many women have worked as regular organizers in their own trades, and a number are still so engaged.

Among the international organizations, widely contrasted as they are in type, some with a large membership and others still small and struggling, there are active and energetic women leaders who have held or still hold official positions in international organizations.

The few names that follow are not chosen with any intention of classifying and appraising the women labor leaders of the day, nor has the list any claim to be complete, or it would be far longer. As one national official remarks of his own union, some of the brightest, most active and influential girls, women displaying high talents for leadership, have exercised their talents, and have achieved success solely in their own localities, many of them perhaps never even coming under the notice of the heads of their organizations. But the fact at least is worth noting that in several trade unions women have been able to forge ahead to positions where they can influence the national councils of the union and represent its policies in the field.

The first woman to hold an executive position in any international union was Augusta Lewis (New York), who was elected corresponding secretary of the International Typographical Union in 1870. The men mention with pride that she was a woman of ability, and did credit to

WOMEN IN MODERN TRADE UNIONS 97

the office; she has had, however, no successor of her own sex. Ellen Lindstrom (Chicago), was in 1901 elected member of the General Executive Board of the Special Order Clothing Workers. When in 1902 that organization amalgamated with the United Garment Workers of America, Miss Lindstrom was re-elected to the Board for another year. Other women of the Board of the U. G. W. A. have been Lillian Fredericks (Indianapolis), Margaret Daley (Coney Island, N. Y.) and Mrs. Edith Souter Metz and Mrs. Daisy Houck, both of Los Angeles. The first woman general organizer for any international union was Emma Lamphere, Retail Clerk (1904).

Mrs. Sara Conboy (Boston) has been since her election in 1915 Secretary-Treasurer of the Textile Workers.

The Boot and Shoe Workers' Union, of whom about thirty per cent of the members are women, have always one woman on the Board. Those who have been elected are Mary A. Nason, Emma Steghagen, Mary Anderson and Clara Katzor.

Elizabeth Maloney, waitress (Chicago), was from 1914 until her death in 1921 a very active member of the Executive Board of the Hotel and Restaurant Employes. Her place was taken by Kitty Donnelly (Cleveland). Miss Mary McEnerney, bookbinder (Chicago), was on the Executive Board of the International Brotherhood of Bookbinders.

Now (1923), Julia O'Connor is President of the Telephone Operators' Department of the International Brotherhood of Electrical Workers. Fannia Cohn is one of the Vice-Presidents of the International Ladies' Garment Workers and Secretary of the Educational Department.

Agnes Nestor has been both President and Secretary-Treasurer of the International Glove Workers Union, and

Elisabeth Christman has been Secretary-Treasurer for some years.

Women are also on other boards. Mary E. Meehan, Anna Neary and Augusta J. Frincke, International Brotherhood of Bookbinders; Mary E. Moran, Laundry Workers International Union; Ethel E. Tulloch, National Union of Postoffice Clerks; Helen Cahill and Nora Long, Upholsterers.

Agnes Johnson is organizer for the Boot and Shoe Workers, and Mary Dempsey till recently, for the Hotel and Restaurant Employes.

Mamie Santora (Baltimore) is on the General Executive Board of the Amalgamated Clothing Workers of America.

The National Women's Trade Union League Convention in 1917, and again in 1919, asked the American Federation of Labor and all of its constituent bodies to guarantee to women workers adequate representation by women responsible to their organizations on all policy making councils, bureaus, boards or committees that deal with conditions of employment or standards of life. Especially do women trade unionists desire representation upon the Executive Council of the American Federation of Labor itself. The Council consists of the officers and eight vice-presidents, belonging to different international unions, but all men, with no possible chink in sight through which a woman could unobserved creep into a seat.

Trade union women consider that on the whole they are at a disadvantage in being granted but limited opportunities for holding positions of responsibility. At the St. Paul Convention of the American Federation of Labor in 1918, the women delegates brought in an amendment to the constitution increasing the number of vice-presidents to ten, with the additional proviso that at least two members of the entire council should be women.

WOMEN IN MODERN TRADE UNIONS

This was countered by the argument that to ask for two women representatives was essentially undemocratic. "Why," said some, "women can fill any or all of the seats now if the delegates choose to elect them." The women not unnaturally felt that two birds in the hand would be worth many in the bush. The amendment passed into the charge of the Constitution Committee, who reported non-concurrence. The Convention adopted the report and the incident was closed—for the time.

There is another matter which the women persist in bringing to the attention of the American Federation of Labor, and that is the refusal of some organizations to take in women members.

The principle of autonomy for the different organized trades on which the American Federation of Labor is based, has other by-results besides self-government and self-control for the member organizations in the management of their own affairs. One of these is seen in the difficulty the Federation sometimes experiences in putting into practice its own principles of unity in the labor movement, without regard to race, color or sex.

There are certain of the international organizations which set up bars against admission to membership, even although the applicant is actually working at the trade.

The United Brotherhood of Carpenters and Joiners, the Journeyman Barbers' International Union, and the International Molders' Union absolutely refuse to admit women, closing their eyes to the fact that women are undercutting men in the furniture factories, where they can be hired for lower wages than men; that women are helping to disorganize the hairdresser's occupation, when against their will they are compelled to remain outside the organization, with the standard conditions that regulate the union barber's shop, and that women core makers in foundries ought to have union protection and be working on union terms.

The men's arguments are of the most plausible character. Their particular job is always "unfit for women." A pressman once seriously argued that feeding is not work for a girl, and nearly collapsed when overalls were suggested as attire sufficiently modest to meet any contingency of the press-room. (That was in pre-war days, but his tribe are to be met in almost every workshop in a number of trades.) The teamsters will not agree to admit a woman, even though she be driving a jitney and competing for fares with the chauffeur carrying his union card.

The hopeful aspect for the future lies in inconsistency of practice. Take the Metal Trades. The International Molders' Union have in the constitution a clause under which "Any member, honorary or active, who devotes his time in whole or in part to the instruction of female help in the foundry, or in any branch of the trade, shall be expelled from the union." The International Metal Polishers' Union, while earnestly discouraging women from entering the trade, on the ground of the danger of contracting tuberculosis, through inhaling the flying metallic or emery dust, admits women to full membership, and insists on equal pay for all women employed in a union shop. This holds everywhere, except in the state of New York. The International Brotherhood of Foundry Employes, on the other hand, admit women, and during the war, at least, had a number of women members in different parts of the country. The Amalgamated Sheet Metal Workers' International Alliance and the International Association of Machinists both admit women, although on a reduced dues and benefit basis. Even although the war broke down many vocational barriers, Article IX, Section 1 of the constitution, "Any boy engaging himself to learn the trade of a machinist must serve four years" probably throws insuperable difficulties in the way of women becoming highly skilled, all-round machinists.

If from metal we turn to wood, while the United Brotherhood of Carpenters and Joiners do not admit women in their order, there is the International Union of Timber Workers, a small organization which holds all female workers in the timber industry eligible to membership, and in wartime reported having several thousand members.

Here are national organizations, employed in practically one industry, handling the question in very different ways. Which is the right solution? Which will be the permanent one?

One way of partly overcoming the difficulty is for the American Federation of Labor to exercise its undoubted right to live up to its own principles of shutting out from the labor movement no one on account of color, sex, nationality or creed. The Federation has large jurisdictional powers. It can ignore the recalcitrant internationals, and issue federal charters to locals of women, thus bringing them within the labor movement, giving them its protection, and taking away any excuse for being undercutters or strike-breakers. This plan would not interfere with trade autonomy, and yet it would go some distance towards abolishing a situation full of danger to all workers, and most humiliating to women.

Owing to the influence of a group of women outside the labor movement, and as a result of their desire that justice should be done to women, the subject was brought before the A. F. of L. Convention in Denver, in 1921, being introduced by Delegate Ethel Haig, tobacco-worker. Her request took the form of an amendment to the constitution, but all that involved was this same question of granting **separate** federal charters. The resolution was decently buried under the folds of a substitute resolution calling upon those national and international organizations that do not admit women workers to "give early consideration for such admission."

A few days only before these happenings, the Executive Board of the National Woman's Trade Union League, meeting in Waukegan, Illinois, appointed a committee to confer with the Executive Council of the American Federation of Labor with reference to the issue of charters to groups of women not admitted to membership in the international unions of their trade. The Committee met with the Council in Atlantic City on August 23, 1921.

The Committee when it met with the Council asked if the A. F. of L. did not in fact determine the jurisdictional lines when national charters were issued, and if it did not subsequently adjust jurisdictional disputes, even to the extent of carving out new jurisdictions. This was done in the case of the ordnance men who were taken out of the National Federation of Federal Employes, and given a local charter. One of the cases troubling the women at present is that of copy-holders who work in union printing offices, and yet, unless they have served the regular printer's apprenticeship, are not eligible to admission into the International Typographical Union.

The case of colored workers was brought up, but the Council refused to take as a precedent affecting the women's status the action of the Montreal Convention. On that occasion the Convention did agree to issue separate charters to colored locals in trades where the international, after having been applied to, refused to take them in.

The discussion closed on the understanding that there would be further negotiation with the Council, and Mr. Gompers suggested conferences with those international bodies which still exclude women.

At the Convention of the Federation in 1922 in Cincinnati, the subject again came up, at the instance of the fraternal delegate of the National Women's Trade Union League, Mrs. Mary V. Halas. The decision of the convention, which was unanimous, was that where women are refused admission by the international of their trade, the Executive Council of the A. F. of L. shall take up the subject with the trade unions involved, and endeavor to reach an understanding as to issuance of federal charters.

The labor movement is being strengthened by the unprecedented activity taking place among the workingmen's wives. This is seen in the rapid growth of women's auxiliaries and their enlarged program of work. For many years a number of the national organizations, such as the Letter Carriers, the Machinists, the Milk Wagon Drivers, the Post Office Clerks, the Railway Mail Clerks and the Switchmen have had national women's auxiliaries. The size of the membership, the number of lodges or locals, and the activities carried on have varied widely from time to time. The care of sick or stranded men, the maintenance of social family relations between the members, holding meetings or entertainments to stimulate the life of the main organization and pride in its achievements, were among their duties. Especially at convention time in a convention city the women's auxiliary might be expected to come to the front. Beside the national bodies, women's auxiliaries have sprung up locally.

During the last few years there has been a rebirth of the spirit in which such organizations originated. Locally this has shown itself in the numberless women's auxiliaries organized in connection with the miners and railway men's strikes and lock-outs. These bodies have been of the new type, formed primarily to strengthen the union. In one bakers' strike the women picketed where the men were absolutely prevented from doing so. In the strike of the Boston City Police, the large meetings held by the women were among the most effective means of reaching the public. Such activities as these mean the education of the women, and the enlisting of their intelligent co-operation by the union officers. Home-keeping women are working also on the lines of more formal education, a women's auxiliary being an active supporter of classes in connection with one of the trade union colleges.

It was the National Women's Auxiliary of the Post-Office Clerks which was able to break through the administrative barriers which for so long prevented the postal employes from having their salaries re-classified by Congress, by bringing the many unfavorable discriminations against these Government employes, previously unknown, as well as the insanitary conditions under which many of them worked, before the public, and at length before Congress. The women's success in connection with all these matters has been very remarkable.

Women have always voluntarily and involuntarily played an indispensable part in the general labor movement, and in backing labor policies, as directed and carried out by men, for men's organizations. In every strike and lockout, in every wage cut, it is the woman at home who pays a large proportion of the price, in an empty coal-box, a shortage of milk for the baby, of clothes and of shoes for the children and herself. If there is an eviction, it is not the man alone that is turned out into the street. If she understands the cause of the struggle, the principle that is fought for, the woman will be a far more valuable helper.

There is another side to this question. If the woman at home has to pay so dearly, and if not only submission and endurance, but sympathy and active co-operation are expected of her, then why not grant her a say in the calling of the strike, in its settlement or in its calling-off? The women's auxiliaries seem to offer a way to reach the women for just such expression of opinion. As long as the home women are related to the labor movement only through their personal relation to husband, brother or son, the connection must often be a loose and temporary one. If the women relatives of the men in every local union had an actively functioning auxiliary it would be possible, and even be easy for the men to consult and advise with the women most closely concerned. This method would also give to the women the tardy justice of a vote upon decisions which so intimately touch themselves. The union man's wife would not longer be in the position which she holds today of being able to vote on a political issue while she is denied a vote on industrial and economic issues.

CHAPTER VI

A NEW DEVELOPMENT IN ORGANIZATION—THE WOMEN'S TRADE UNION LEAGUE

After the Civil War there came the period of reconstruction, and after that an awakening of the social conscience, manifested in many ways. There was the establishment of state care for the insane, the blind, and the poor to replace voluntary organization. There were the tenement house investigations, the social settlement movement, the eight hour movement. Miss Grace Dodge's work in forming working women's clubs had its influence. In the political field was the populist movement, the activities of the Socialist Party and the propaganda of the single taxers.

All these efforts were influenced by the working class movement and every form of social advance on the other hand helped to release the workers' energies. In the early nineties amid the often disheartening struggles of both international and local unions, there was a widespread sense of unrest with a background of keen dissatisfaction among the intelligent workers herded in sweatshops and crowding the poorer districts of all large cities. Here and there were the signs of struggle and of effort towards a coming together. Some fine spirited women, not of the exploited class, began to associate themselves with the women workers to strengthen their cause. In New York, Boston and Chicago, we find the women workers allied with other women sympathetic with labor and thus encouraged to concerted effort.

THE WOMEN'S TRADE UNION LEAGUE 107

In New York, Boston and Chicago, women of the type of Josephine Shaw Lowell, Lillian Wald, Mrs. Mary Morton Kehew and Jane Addams, were bringing a new spirit into our city life. Through knowledge gained of city and community evils they were learning of the many injustices that were perpetrated upon the worker, upon the immigrant, upon the colored race and upon the woman, especially the young girl. These girl workers were many of them so young that they ought to have been covered by child labor laws, child labor laws that did not then exist. Women therefore came forward to see what, if any, contribution they could make towards filling up a gap in the labor movement.

In 1892, Miss Mary Kenney, a young bookbinder (now Mrs. Mary Kenney O'Sullivan), it will be recalled, was organizing for the American Federation of Labor.

In Chicago she discovered in Mrs. Charles Henrotin an early and loyal friend in the struggle for the industrial betterment of the downtrodden working women. Hull House threw open its rooms for meetings held in the unpopular cause of bringing working women together, and enrolling them in trade unions. Shortly after a women's Federal Labor Union was formed. Active in this agitation were Mrs. Fannie Kavanagh Stanton, Miss Lizzie Ford, Mrs. T. J. Morgan, Mrs. Frank J. Pearson, Mrs. Robert Howe, Dr. Fannie Dickinson, Mrs. Florence Kelley and Mrs. Corinne Brown.

The effect of training in the Knights of Labor was seen here, for Mrs. Alzina P. Stevens, originally a textile worker, Mrs. George Rodgers and Miss Emma Steghagen, boot and shoe worker, who had all three been members of the Knights of Labor, brought their experience to the aid of the girls who were forming local unions. Among this group also Miss Kenney was a leader. She not only reached girls in her own trade (bookbinding) but garment workers and shoe workers and others, including numbers of men.

Mr. Gompers then sent Miss Kenney to the East. When in Boston, Miss Hannah Kimball, and later her sister, Mrs. Mary M. Kehew, encouraged to the utmost her efforts to organize women into trade unions. The first thing she did was to form a big club, called the Union of Industrial Progress. Their musical evenings were made stirring with labor songs.

Mary Kenney with her witching Irish personality gathered the girls together for social evenings with dancing, music and games as the attraction, and little talks on industrial matters tactfully sandwiched in.

The great difficulty Miss Kenney and others experienced was that it was almost impossible to make anyone, even working women, understand what was meant, for they did not realize that women were within the scope of the labor movement.

In Boston a Federal Labor Union used to meet at Denison House, the college settlement. The union had been organized by John F. O'Sullivan, and was regularly affiliated with the American Federation of Labor, and even sent George E. McNeil as its delegate to one A. F. of L. convention. Its membership was not confined to working women. The union took in such women as Mary Morton Kehew, Emily Balch, Vida Scudder, Helen Dudley, Hannah P. Kimball, Rose Lamb, and Anne Withington, names always associated with labor's struggles. There were many unhappy adventures with strikes, for the women were almost wholly unorganized.

The union took part also in forwarding the labor legislation of that day. At that time there would be only two or three persons at a labor legislation hearing, while today the hearings are packed. John F. O'Sullivan was in many ways a remarkable man. He had the most profound belief in women and the little Federal Labor Union was his pride and joy.

It was in this environment somewhat later that the National Women's Trade Union League had its beginnings. The League traces its origin, however, to the year 1873, when Mrs. Emma Paterson, an Englishwoman, was visiting New York. She was the daughter of a schoolmaster and the wife of a cabinet maker, himself a trade unionist. While in New York she saw and was impressed by the activities of certain local organizations managed by women, such as the Parasol and Umbrella Makers' Union, the Women's Typographical Union, and the Working Women's Protective Union. On her return to England Mrs. Paterson and some of her friends organized the Women's Protective and Provident League. It was not until later that the name British Women's Trade Union League was adopted. The object was to aid in organizing women into trade unions, and it drew support both from men's trade unions and from thoughtful women who were not themselves workers. Although this League was founded in 1874, there was nothing known about it in the United States till about 1903. The pioneer activities of the Englishwomen were observed by Mr. William English Walling when he was paying a visit to England. Mr. Walling spoke to Mrs. O'Sullivan. At a little Boston downtown restaurant they talked over the possibilities of forming such an organization here, having asked in Mrs. Kehew and Miss Emily Balch to help. A meeting was arranged, Mr. Walling taking the lead. At the American Federation of Labor Convention just being held in Boston, Mr. Gompers gave Mrs. O'Sullivan permission to announce the meeting from the platform. Mr. Walling and Mrs. O'Sullivan sent telegrams to Jane Addams, Mary McDowell and Lillian Wald, asking them to act on the Executive Board of the new organization. The result has already been related in "The Trade Union Woman."

A meeting of those interested was called in Faneuil Hall on November 14, 1903. Mr. John O'Brien, President of the Retail Clerks' International Protective Union, presided. Among the trades represented were the Ladies' Garment Workers, the United Garment Workers, the Amalgamated Meat Cutters and Butcher Workmen, Retail Clerks, Shoe Workers, and Textile Workers. The National Women's Trade Union League was organized and the following officials elected: President, Mrs. Mary Morton Kehew, Boston; Vice-President, Miss Jane Addams, Chicago; Secretary, Mrs. Mary Kenney O'Sullivan, Boston; Treasurer, Miss Mary Donovan, Boot and Shoe Workers; members, Miss M. McDowell, Chicago, Miss Lillian D. Wald, New York; Miss Ellen Lindstrom, United Garment Workers, Miss Mary Freitas, Textile Workers, and Miss Leonora O'Reilly, Ladies' Garment Workers.

Prominent trade unionists active in these forward steps were Mr. Max Morris, (Retail Clerks) a Vice-President of the American Federation of Labor, John Tobin, President of the Boot and Shoe Workers, James Tansey, President of the United Textile Workers, Harry White, President of the United Garment Workers, and Michael Donnelly, President of the Amalgamated Meat Cutters and Butcher Workmen. The British fraternal delegates to the A. F. of L. Convention bore witness to the effective work already accomplished by the British Women's Trade Union League.

The following year branches were established in New York, Boston and Chicago. Gertrude Barnum, as first national organizer did effective work first in Massachusetts, (where the Fall River strike hit the textile workers very hard), by making the facts known through the daily press of the country. In the same way she aided in the Troy Laundry Workers' strike, as well as in the lock-out of the corset workers of Aurora, Illinois.

THE WOMEN'S TRADE UNION LEAGUE 111

The establishment of the National Women's Trade Union League and its local branches was a new development. It created for the first time within the American labor movement what was practically a federation of trade unions with women members. It recognized and induced others to recognize the working women's group as sharing in the problems and difficulties common to all, yet also with problems of their own, problems for which it was necessary to find a solution.

The leaders of the new movement have directed their energies into two or three distinct channels. Their ultimate aim is to concentrate and give unified expression to the aims and aspirations of the working women whether these are waitresses or seamstresses, paper box makers or telegraphers. Their immediate purpose is to build up and strengthen the trade union membership by aiding organization wherever they see the need, sometimes directly, more often by giving help to local unions already in existence.

Where organization is too slow a method to relieve oppression, it is on legislation that the League bends its efforts. The work is still in the experimental stage, but the very fact that so important and representative a group of labor women have come together, and are expressing their common desires, has placed those desires in more definite form before labor men. The men have realized more clearly how reasonable the women's demands are, and how urgent it is, for the sake of the whole labor cause, that they be aided in their efforts to raise wage standards and improve the working conditions of the underpaid and overworked women, with whom our factories are filled.

Labor leaders admit that the woman organizer is an indispensable factor if women are to be drawn in in any effective numbers into the trade unions. The practical difficulties in the path of the ordinary man business agent when trying to convert girls to his way of thinking are too great. It is not always easy for a man to win a girl's confidence, nor is he always familiar enough with the details of her job to talk convincingly about it. This shows the need of women organizers, and many of them, drawn from various trades, speaking different languages, and trained both in the technical side of organizing, and in a broad understanding of the relations of the workers to industry.

Further, since men trade unionists have their own hard and pressing problems to face, and are absorbed in these, if men only have the directing of labor policies, either in the national bodies, or in the local unions, or in the American Federation of Labor itself, it will inevitably happen that the affairs of women, and the interests of women will receive much less attention than their importance deserves. The leading women trade unionists in the ranks of the League have therefore been interpreters to the men of the labor movement of the silent discontent, of the unrighted wrongs and of the suppressed irritations of a vast number of working women in many occupations, in many centers. Their task of interpretation is a continuous one, and one which has to be carried to fresh organizations of men as new occupations are opened up to women.

There are modern ways in which trade union men can encourage the entrance of women into the unions. One is to encourage women organizers and to see that a much larger number of women organizers are kept in the field all the time. It must be remembered that although the amount of money which has been expended by the trade unionists of the United States and Canada is very large, the proportion used to bring the women into trade unions is comparatively insignificant.

Another way is by granting to women representation

THE WOMEN'S TRADE UNION LEAGUE

upon all labor bodies, committees and boards, beginning with the Executive Council of the American Federation of Labor, and including the executive boards of all national unions with women members.

The League membership aims:—

To provide a common meeting ground for women of all groups who endorse the principles of democracy and wish to see them applied to industry.

To encourage self-government in the workshop.

To develop leadership among the women workers, inspiring them with a sense of personal responsibility for the conditions under which they work.

To insure the protection of the younger girls in their efforts for better working conditions and a living wage.

To secure for girls and women equal opportunity with boys and men in trades and technical training and pay on the basis of occupation and not on the basis of sex.

To secure the representation of women on industrial tribunals and public boards and commissions.

To interpret to the public generally the aims and purposes of the trade union movement.

To be successful, any association must measure up to the needs of its own time. To do this, it is often necessary to look ahead a little, as the League did, when it asked for a federal enquiry into the conditions under which women were working; when it led in the endeavor to establish within the Department of Labor a Woman's Division under a woman chief; when it urged upon the President of the United States, the Secretary of War, and the Secretary of the Navy, the importance of declaring standards for women's work in wartime; when it sent two of its members to the Peace Conference at Versailles to present its reconstruction program; when, backed by the working women of Great Britain and France, it called the first

International Congress of Working Women. To bring this about the League did not hesitate to lay aside some of its own local duties, expending its resources on making intercommunication between the wage-earning women of widely separated lands a reality and a success.

The important part played by the National Women's Trade Union League in providing a channel of expression and an organization to safeguard in some degree the interests of all women workers was well exemplified during the war. A few years earlier there would have been no such organization in existence. In the chapter dealing with working women and the war there is a brief account of how women in industry were affected through the placing of war orders in this country, from at least the beginning of 1915.

In June, 1917, when the Kansas City Convention was held, our country had already been actually involved in the war for three months, and the problems of women's employment and the work they were being asked to do, needed closer attention than ever on account of the army raised by conscription removing tens of thousands of men from the industries. The convention outlined standards of industry to be established for government contracts, which were presented to President Wilson himself, to Secretary of War Baker, and to Secretary of Labor Wilson, and to the Women in Industry Committee of the Council of National Defense. In many of the states these standards were adopted and also in the United States Ordnance Department.

In the biennial conventions of the League, trade union women have emphasized their stand on vocational training. They feel that it should be co-educational. Any other plan could only prove, later on, an additional handicap to the sex overlooked. They ask also that it include an

THE WOMEN'S TRADE UNION LEAGUE

intelligent knowledge of the development of modern industry, showing why collective bargaining is a necessity, and also some knowledge of labor legislation, and the impressing upon the worker of the duty laid upon her to help in the enforcement of laws enacted for her own protection. Trade union women in convention have also pled for the woman on the farm, the economic value of whose product is unquestioned, although it goes unrecognized because she is not paid money wages. Since there is no record of the wealth she creates, she is not regarded as a genuine creator of wealth. In the convention of 1915 these same trade union women asked that women's colleges should throw open their doors to wage-earning women during the slack summer months when it would be possible for the working girl to attend for a summer course. This had its fulfilment first at Bryn Mawr College in the Summer School of 1921.

The National Women's Trade Union League, because it is part of the woman movement as well as a part of organized labor, has often interpreted to labor men the needs of women and has not infrequently passed on to them the inspiration of women's idealism. It has besides welded additional links only too much needed between the working class movement and the woman movement, as expressed through such organizations as the National League of Women Voters and the General Federation of Women's Clubs, the National Young Women's Christian Association and women's colleges. Valuable support also has been accorded by the Federal Council of Churches and the Catholic Welfare Council.

In the year 1907 Mrs. Raymond Robins accepted the position of National President to the then infant league. During the next fifteen years Mrs. Robins put up a record for initiative, courage and resourcefulness. In her public life the cause of the labor women, who had chosen her as their leader, was always her first interest. Not the least of her qualifications as a leader in these difficult days, is that she has vision that helps her to look forward to the claims of tomorrow as well as the needs of today; in this Mrs. Robins has been continually supported by her sister, Miss Mary Dreier.

The local League in New York opened its first headquarters in a small home in one of the East Side streets. A year later, as one of the charter members relates, when a room on First Avenue up five flights of dirty and dark stairs was secured, that was thought to be a great meeting place for working women.

The earliest call made upon them for help was in that most pitiful of all social uprisings, a children's strike. These young strikers, children under twelve, were asking for shorter hours and higher wages. When arrested and brought for picketing before the Jefferson Market Court, members of the League came to their help, and succeeded in attracting some public attention towards their deplorable situation.

It is pathetic as well as ridiculous to recall that it was necessary to provide the children with legal assistance to meet a charge of violent resistance. Children are the hardest group of any to aid. As has been said: "They as a whole want to work, the parents want them to work and the employer wants them to work, so they all unite to dodge the law. Children are unconscious philosophers and stoics. If they are underpaid, overworked, forced to work under conditions which few men or women would stand, they rarely complain but take it all as a matter of course."

Going outside of New York, the League was called to give assistance in the laundry workers' strike in Troy, N. Y., in 1905, described elsewhere.

In New York some young cap-makers went out on a

THE WOMEN'S TRADE UNION LEAGUE 117

strike. They were asking shorter hours and more money. They were also protesting against the custom of having to pay for their own machines, needles, thread and power. Among the cap-makers were a number of Slavic-Jewesses who would work all day and attend lectures and debates at night. One of these was Rose Schneiderman, who first came to the front in this cap-makers' strike. She has been an ardent trade unionist ever since, and is now president of the Women's Trade Union League of New York, and Vice-President of the National League.

Between 1904 and 1909 work was very slow and results apparently but insignificant. But league members kept in touch with the poorest and weakest and searched out yet other poor and weak ones among the hat trimmers, the shirtwaist makers, the petticoat makers, the white goods workers, the neckwear workers, the leather workers, and the textile workers, making friends with individual girls and meeting with them and their friends in halls in the rear of saloons, for no other halls were open to them. They knew nothing of social settlements in those days. League members went out on the streets and talked at street corners, at the hour when the working girls were going home.

In 1909 came the first of the large strikes in the women's trades. It called out the shirtwaist makers in an uprising which has been often described. That strike was the last of a long series and was known at the time as the "Strike of the Forty Thousand." Every morning the League stationed their own members in front of factories to act as witnesses in cases of unlawful arrest and to check the insulting conduct of many of the police. They helped in the provision of bail, provision prompt and adequate; but the greatest contribution and the one in which they themselves gained experience against many and succeeding industrial struggles, was the securing of publicity for the workers in bringing out before churches and clubs and in the newspapers, the intolerable conditions that had driven these young foreign girls to revolt. Were little girls in short skirts given terms in the workhouse, the League leaders had a picture taken of a group of them, each displaying a badge that announced she was a "workhouse prisoner." Of course that was a good picture to print and printed it was. In these and many other like ways the League played a part in the struggle, which, often renewed since, has at length ended in the transformation of the needle trades from a sweated and degraded occupation to one of the best paid, most highly standardized and most efficient trades in the country.

In 1911 occurred the appalling fire in the Triangle Factory in Washington Square. A fire in a new fire-proof building, so surely fire-proof in structure that a few hours after the flames were out the firemen were able to walk across the floors unharmed; yet the corpses of one hundred and forty-three girls, and the injured bodies of many more bore witness to the fact that no fire-proof building spells safety unless the lives of the workers are protected by proper management. The Women's Trade Union League came to the front immediately, organizing a citizens' committee to push for an investigation. The Chicago League and other local leagues followed suit by urging the need for the Fire Prevention Bureaus which have since been established in many cities.

Very similar has been the struggle of the League in other cities. In Boston, garment workers, office building cleaners, telephone girls and news-stand girls, have all been aided in their efforts to build up organizations.

In the strike of policemen, when in 1919 the city was policed by troops and the entire state was wrought up to a high pitch of excitement over the several rights of the state, of the city authorities, the public and the workers the Women's Trade Union League helped to place, through a well-prepared statement, through meetings addressed by well-known citizens and through mass gatherings of the policemen's wives some of the reasons for the men's position.

In Chicago the League's first work, which there dates from 1904, was with the locked out corset workers of Aurora, Illinois; they took what was then quite an original move, by writing to all the women's clubs throughout Illinois, telling the conditions under which were working those women who were making garments for women. They were able to help in the stockyards strike (1904) which involved so many hundreds of girls.

When the general strike in the men's garment trade struck Chicago in the Fall of 1909, the League co-operated with the United Garment Workers and with the Chicago Federation of Labor; especially was it helpful in the share it played in the establishment of commissary stores. The officers also aided both in the making of the settlements which resulted from that strike, particularly the Hart, Schaffner & Marx agreement, and also in the working out of that agreement.

In Philadelphia the League has co-operated in raising standards and furthering the organization of waitresses, women upholsterers, cigar makers, office workers, candy makers, dress makers, neckwear workers, machinists, textile workers, telegraphers, leather workers, librarians and public school teachers.

The criticism had often previously been made of working women that they showed little desire for their political enfranchisement. Through the leagues in the various cities working women gathered together and formed industrial sections of the woman's suffrage movement, carrying on campaigns among working women and labor voters, reaching also vast numbers of working men who were not themselves unionists. In New York, for example, members of the section who spoke Italian used to go down into the subways, then in process of construction, and interested the often astonished Italian workmen busy at their subterranean task. There were even more direct pleas, visits to Albany and Springfield, Illinois, when the legislature was in session, by working girls pleading for suffrage. Nor did these confine their attention to the inhabitants of cities. In trips all over the States of Massachusetts and New York, and especially on automobile tours, working women made a deep impression on the voters, distributing literature of an original type, urging many most practical arguments and influencing definitely the up-state or down-state working class vote.

In the Fall of 1913 the National Women's Trade Union League established a small training school for women planning to do active work in the labor movement as organizers, secretaries or investigators. It was the first full-time labor school in this country, and is still, we believe, the only one giving field training as well as academic work.

The school gives instruction in English, public speaking, in labor problems and the handling of meetings. The students learn to draft a trade union agreement and through field work handle the practical problems of the organizer. From small beginnings the school is gradually extending its work, and indirectly its influence has been felt in the recent developments of the workers' education, such as the Bryn Mawr summer school for women in industry.

The local leagues co-operate wherever there is an effort to establish workers' education.

THE WOMEN'S TRADE UNION LEAGUE 121

In many difficult situations the National Women's Trade Union League and its local branches have helped the women workers to gain the victory or in the midst of defeat to snatch advantages for the future building up of their organization. This has been notably so in the long struggle in the needle trades, where it contributed everything that an organization could for a number of years. The assistance of its organizers has been time and again at the disposal of every needle trades union. To the United Garment Workers it contributed the services of Mary Anderson and Bessie Abramovitch (now Mrs. Sidney Hillman), educating the women in meeting shop difficulties in the early days of the Hart, Schaffner & Marx agreement.

In New York Rose Schneiderman for four years gave aid to the International Ladies' Garment Workers, working among the unorganized white goods workers.

To the then almost untouched South went Mary Thompson in the textile mills, and Mildred Rankin and Bertha Funk made the colored workers of Norfolk their care.

Mrs. Maud Swartz, printer, was elected National President in 1922.

During the nearly twenty years of its existence the League and its branches have been associated with working women in the most varied occupations; its membership has been drawn from among every branch of the sewing trades; from textile workers, workers in metal, paper, paint, celluloid and food products. Manicurists and scrub women, soap makers and printers, stockyards workers, jewelry workers, household workers, hospital employes, public health nurses and office workers, are some others, that make up the great army of women who have been drawn into contact with this organization, and who have helped to build up its membership.

The connection of the League with the setting on foot

of the agitation for an investigation into the conditions of wage-earning women and children, which had as its culmination the establishment of the Women's Bureau, is described in the chapter so entitled.

The National Women's Trade Union League stands for placing industry upon such a basis that the long and exhausting strikes of which we have so many, shall be made unnecessary; made unnecessary through such organization of the workers that industry can be placed upon an equitable basis and the collective agreement and not force or individual profit be the deciding factor in any industrial arrangement or re-arrangement. That the workers may be strong to meet difficulties, and wise in facing them, is the argument for organization and for education with women as well as men.

Chapter VII

INDUSTRIAL LEGISLATION

The field of industrial legislation is large and covers such laws as the limitation of hours, the forbidding or regulating of night work, controlling the payment of wages, either as to amount or the form in which they must be paid, the time at which they may be paid, notice of discharge, deductions from wages, whether as fines or in any other form.

Inside the factory working conditions may be the subject of legislative action, usually of state laws, often of city ordinances. The health and endurance of employes and their liability through lowered resistance to succumb to disease, are matters of great importance to the workers, and hence, it must be remembered, to the community. Therefore temperature must be regulated; and ventilation, the getting rid of used air, the drawing off of excessive heat and humidity, and its replacement by pure and fresh air, is equally important. When we touch upon industries in which the air is vitiated by far more dangerous elements than the breath or other exhalations of the human body, the regulation of these matters has to be yet more definite and precise. From this we go on to enter the field of occupational disease. Lead, for instance, is in use in more than one hundred trades and in some forms is most injurious to the worker. If yellow phosphorus is employed in making matches, it is likely to cause decay of the jaw in those who handle it. Mercury will poison those who work with it. Dust in the air given off in grinding stone or metals, or in the form of powdered flint, is very harmful to the lungs and may be the basis of many respiratory troubles. Some of these are very ancient types of injury and are mentioned, so says Dr. Alice Hamilton, as occurring as far back as the Roman Empire.

Again, many of the diseases that today take a heavy toll of the workers' strength and of many workers' lives, are entirely the result of our modern industrial system of making everything on a great scale, of utilizing machinery to the limit and of turning to commercial use the marvelous discoveries of the last hundred years in the field of applied chemistry. The nervous exhaustion and the hazards to health that follow in the train of night work had no existence till modern systems of lighting began to be installed in manufacturing plants. The hand tools and the simple machinery of times as recent as the eighteenth century held few risks for the artisan. The individual wielder of the chisel and the hammer could very well care for his own safety. The spinner and the weaver inhaled little fine lint from the atmosphere they breathed. The scant use of artificial light in former days largely limited to the hours of daylight any work that was trying to the eyes.

We were altogether unprepared for the development of new industrial health risks during the World War. The unfamiliar chemicals, and especially the high explosives and poison gases, never before known in human history, brought death and destruction to many outside of their intended field among the unfortunate human beings who chanced to be on the firing line or within the danger limits of the battle on either side of the conflict. Inasmuch as these instruments of death were incredibly more powerful and ruinous to the enemy than any weapon of warfare hitherto

INDUSTRIAL LEGISLATION

conceived of by man, so inevitably was their manufacture attended by greater risks. Furthermore, these risks were many of them unforeseen, even by the chemists who invented the compounds. Much less did the manufacturer who produced them or the working people who handled them, suspect them as the cause of illness and death.

Trinitrotoluol, or TNT, was the most dangerous of these compounds, causing in Great Britain during 1916-17 370 cases of toxic jaundice with 96 deaths, and in the United States no less than 13 known deaths more than a year before our entrance into the war. Less dangerous to life but causing distressing affections of the skin were tetryl, picric acid and fulminate of mercury. The girls who worked with them suffered from burning, itching eruptions, the disfiguring effect of which was added to by a dirty yellow or orange stain of the skin, hair and eyebrows, a stain which lasted months after the girl had left work. Ether was used in the manufacture of smokeless powder, and the girls and women who worked in the ether fumes experienced the acute discomfort attendant upon the early stages of ether anaesthesia, headache, throbbing, nausea, thirst, vomiting, excitement, then depression and drowsiness followed by sleep from which they awoke to all the wretchedness of the after effects of the anaesthesia. Girls were found to be so much more susceptible than men that in Great Britain latterly men alone were employed on the ether work but in the United States they were in it till the end.

Finally, the greatest danger to which workers in American explosive plants were subjected came from the nitrogen oxide gases formed in making gun cotton, picric acid, TNT and tetryl. There were almost 1,400 cases of gassing from this source during 1916, and 28 deaths. The men who breathed these fumes died exactly as did the gassed soldiers in the trenches, or, like them, lived with damaged lungs.

It is a curious commentary upon our lack of foresight and our strange sense of irresponsibility where human welfare is at stake, that in almost all cases the only test that is demanded of a new substance put to use in industry, of a new process adopted by industry, is whether it is materially efficient; that is, whether it will result in production in the amount that is required and at a price that will pay. That is all we ask of the chemist when he turns out a new drug, a new dye or a new war gas. With these conditions he must comply or he cannot market his discovery.

The history of the handling of these novel ingredients in chemical production is on the other hand a story of experiment, with the worker this time, not the material, as the subject of experiment. The knowledge of risks to the munition worker in the use of picric acid, of TNT, of tetryl or of airplane varnish, was not sold along with the secrets of their preparation or combination. That there were such risks was discovered by chemists or by doctors only after the injury had been done and after many groups of workers had suffered.

A most essential addition, therefore, to every manufacturing plant today is a first aid station, perhaps more than one. A certain amount of industrial risk is now recognized as inseparable from the use of these as yet unfamiliar forces that we have drawn into the service of modern industry, and the doctor and the nurse are the agents of protection.

The modern fire hazard is something of which our grandfathers knew nothing. The risks come in all sorts of ways, through our prodigal use of all sorts of inflammable or explosive substances, such as spirituous solvents or celluloid, or gases. The crowding together of immense numbers

INDUSTRIAL LEGISLATION

of men and women may not be insanitary, if adequate ventilation be provided for, but their rescue in case of fire is rendered more difficult with each additional story. Hence the comparative frequency of fatal accidents in the small plants operating in loft buildings of city districts. Escape is far more difficult than in case of fire in a plant of apparently a more dangerous kind, built on the outskirts of a city with greater floor space and of lesser height. It was not until the investigations of the New York State Factory Commission in 1911-13 that public attention was called to this very elementary fact. Mr. H. F. J. Porter, fire expert, explained it thus:

> Buildings occupied by many people on each floor are universally deficient in stairways. The condition has come about through the gradual growth of industry. Small factories had increased the number of their employes and added extensions to their buildings to accommodate them, but provided no additional stairways. Architects and builders, instead of recognizing this defect in their building design, continued blindly to follow the lines which they saw developing. They still designed their buildings with inadequate interior stairways and exit facilities, and then proceeded to develop this outside fire escape into a permanent feature.

Mr. Porter lays it down that a stairway three feet wide to serve a number of floors can accommodate but twelve people per floor above the seventh floor. He and most other fire experts look upon elevator service as worse than useless in case of fire, since an elevator may so easily be blocked and go out of commission, and if blocked between floors during a fire only adds a fresh horror.

Yet another field of industrial legislation is that of workmen's compensation, which comes in the train of the increasing risks, both from accidents and disease, incurred in following modern industrial occupations. These, as we have seen, are likely, with changing methods in manufacture, to increase and appear in new forms. Workmen's compensation laws lay part, at least, of the money cost upon industry, to be met as a regular outlay, part of the overhead expenses of running a business.

Far the larger part of labor legislation affects men equally with women. Certain laws, it is true, such as those regarding sailors or railway engineers, or foremen, or train conductors, bear upon men's condition only, as only men follow those callings. Certain others, again, such as those providing care for women before and after childbirth, or while nursing young infants, are similarly for the benefit of one sex only. There are also a number of laws which for one reason or another, are framed to cover women alone, although their provisions are also desirable for men. The peculiar restrictions of our United States Constitution and of practically all of the state constitutions, introduce a complication which other countries have not to face. But other countries as well as ourselves, have inherited from simpler times and from a simple theory of individual liberty matching those times, the idea that all such questions were fitly to be settled on the basis of a personal bargain between the workman and his employer. Our own peculiar handicap lies in this, that the idea was given such definite and unalterable expression in the federal and state constitutions that though social conditions altered, it was not possible to alter or modify the phraseology of these documents so that practice should keep pace with changing conditions. Efforts to put upon these articles of political and national faith a modern interpretation, have been blocked continuously, blocked through habits of thought, blocked still more effectually by economic interest.

Generation after generation of workers have been sacrificed through this clinging to a literal interpretation of a fine idea, where a spiritual interpretation would have given to it a broader meaning and won from it splendid results for real freedom.

From the year 1847 on, the story of legislative efforts was a most disheartening one. The year 1847 saw the passage in New Hampshire of a bill making a ten-hour day for both men and women the legal workday. Other states followed. The bills carried, nevertheless, what we have come to know later as a joker. The law was not valid in any case where an "express contract" to the contrary, existed between employer and worker. Three days before the law was to come into operation, the manufacturers saw to it that "express contracts" were prepared and signed by the employes.

In the following year the question led to a strike in seven of the cotton factories of Allegheny, Pennsylvania, lasting for seven weeks. The owners then introduced a ten-hour system, but with an accompanying reduction of wages of ten per cent. This compromise the workers accepted in the hope that later wages would be raised "after the next legislature perfects the law, and the manufacturers discover that they can afford it." The law soon fell into disuse. The present ten-hour law of Pennsylvania applies to women only.

In 1852 in the State of Ohio a ten-hour law for all workers was passed, but it again was effective only when the employe was "compelled" to work longer. No really direct compulsion was required when a woman had her bread to earn. It was not necessary for a foreman to stand over her with a whip. The pressing need for employment and the inability to refuse it whatever the terms offered, provided compulsion enough.

In the year 1876 Massachusetts, a state with a great legislative record, standing at the head of all the industrial states in humane legislation concerning the workers, passed a law prohibiting the employment of women and children in manufacture longer than ten hours in one day and 60 hours in one week. The law was tested before the Supreme Court of Massachusetts in 1879, and declared valid.

The State of New York made several similar attempts but no legislation of any value was passed till 1898.

A very serious backward step was taken in Illinois in the celebrated Ritchie case. A law had been passed in 1893, giving women and girls an eight-hour day and a 48-hour week, but two years afterwards it was declared unconstitutional by the Supreme Court of Illinois. This put legislation back for more than ten years.

A new stage was reached when in 1908 came the test case in which the Oregon women's ten-hour law came before the Supreme Court of the United States. The chief agent in making this test case possible was the National Consumers' League of which Miss Josephine Goldmark was research secretary. Miss Goldmark and Mr. Louis D. Brandeis (now Mr. Justice Brandeis on the bench of the United States Supreme Court) prepared a brief in which the law was defended as a health measure, the importance of woman's maternal function being dwelt upon.

The same arguments maintained in the year 1910 the validity of the Illinois ten-hour law for women. Since then, in 1915, the United States Supreme Court on similar grounds declared constitutional the California eight-hour law.

The position of the woman worker as regards what has been known as the "right to leisure" can be seen in the table, which gives a rough summary of legislation in existence in March, 1923, touching weekly hours, daily hours, prohibition of night work, of home work, one day rest in seven and the minimum wage and mothers' pensions. The table gives the general idea only of the state laws. No two states are exactly the same and not one has all the legal protections on its statute books. The legislation affects in some states manufacturing operations only; in others, all workers except in specified industries or occupations, such as graduate nurses or those employed in the canning industries or omits by default domestic employes or agricultural workers. Night work may be prohibited from ten to six, from eleven to six, from ten to seven, after six or after nine. The prohibition of home work may or may not apply to immediate members of the family; may apply to the making and finishing of garments, or may equally forbid home work on the making of cigars and cigarettes; or may consistently banish from the home such occupations as nut picking or the handling of other articles of food.

The minimum wage decrees have ranged anywhere from $8.50 in 1915 to $18.00 in 1921. The wage decrees vary from state to state and from occupation to occupation. They rose with the cost of living during the war and in 1922 they began to drop. The minimum wage in different trades is usually determined by a wage board in that trade, although sometimes a state industrial commission may have power to interpret the law and declare by formal decision what the legal wage shall be, and to what industries it shall apply. In two states the law has prescribed a flat rate.

The mother's pension is in Iowa and Vermont but $2.00 per week for one child; in Florida and Nevada $25.00 a month. In some states only the widowed mother can receive such aid. Elsewhere, those who are divorced, or whose husbands are in prison or who have deserted their families. One year or five of residence in the county may be a necessary preliminary to obtaining a pension. Citizen-

132 WOMEN AND THE LABOR MOVEMENT

TABLE*

SHOWING INDUSTRIAL LEGISLATION AFFECTING WOMEN
MARCH, 1923

State	Hours daily	Hours weekly	One day rest in seven	Night work laws	Home work laws	Minimum wage laws	Mothers' pension
Alabama							
Alaska							yes
Arkansas	9	54	yes			yes	yes
Arizona	8	56				yes	yes
California	8	48	yes	yes		yes	yes
Colorado	8					yes	yes
Connecticut	10	55		yes	yes		yes
Delaware	10	55	yes	yes			yes
Dist. of Columbia	8	48	yes			yes	
Florida							yes
Georgia	10	60					
Idaho	9						yes
Illinois	10				yes		yes
Indiana				yes	yes		yes
Iowa							yes
Kansas	9	49½	yes	yes		yes	yes
Kentucky	10	60					
Louisiana	10	60					yes
Maine	9	54					yes
Maryland	10	60		yes	yes		yes
Massachusetts	9	48	yes	yes	yes	yes	yes
Michigan	9	54			yes		yes
Minnesota	9	54				yes	yes
Mississippi	10	60					
Missouri	9	54			yes		yes
Montana	8						yes
Nebraska	9	54		yes			yes
Nevada	8	56					yes
New Hampshire	10¼	54		yes			yes
New Jersey	10	54	yes		yes		yes

INDUSTRIAL LEGISLATION

State	Hours daily	Hours weekly	One day rest in seven	Night work laws	Home work laws	Minimum wage laws	Mothers' pension
New Mexico	8						
New York	9	54	yes	yes	yes		yes
North Carolina	11	60					
North Dakota	8½	48	yes			yes	yes
Ohio	9	50	yes	yes	yes		yes
Oklahoma	9	54					yes
Oregon	9	48	yes	yes		yes	yes
Pennsylvania	10	54	yes	yes	yes		yes
Rhode Island	10	54					
South Carolina	10	55		yes			
South Dakota	10						yes
Tennessee	10½	57			yes		yes
Texas	9	54					yes
Utah	8	48				yes	yes
Vermont	10½	56					yes
Virginia	10	60					yes
Washington	8		yes			yes	yes
West Virginia							yes
Wisconsin	10	55		yes	yes	yes	yes
Wyoming	10	60					yes
Porto Rico	8	48		yes		yes	

* It is impossible to summarize accurately the state industrial legislation for the reason that so many of the laws apply to certain occupations only or admit of certain exceptions. A state may have a ten-hour law and yet be so limited in its application that students and statisticians will differ as to whether the state ought to be listed as a ten-hour law state or not. The summary here lists the states according to the interpretation of the Women's Bureau. Each state is listed according to the hours that apply to the greatest number of women. The table has been corrected up to March 1, 1923. Readers who wish to know exactly what are the laws of each particular state in accurate detail are referred to Bulletin No. 16 of the Women's Bureau, Washington, D. C. 1921.

ship or pending citizenship may be a condition. It may seem strange to classify mothers' pensions as industrial legislation, but there is no law which can more radically affect the economic condition of the married working woman with children for whom she has to provide a home and up-bringing.

The ultimate aim of all industrial legislation is to standardize industry. In every case where this is attempted by legislation it will be found that an employer here and there, sometimes many employers, with either a wise regard for their own interest, a conscientious sense of responsibility towards their workers, a civic spirit, or a wholesome liking for efficient and orderly methods of work to be carried on by healthy, intelligent and competent workers, have already put into practice the improvement demanded by workers in other plants. Such men usually approve of, and sometimes actively support and advocate legalizing such standards. They know that they are often inconvenienced and embarrassed by the poor employer whose sole idea of economy is to have the burden of saved expense borne by the workers. Although in the end shorter hours and good working conditions are found to be the truest economy, still the incompetent or conscienceless competitor can for a time do a great deal of harm by degrading a whole industry or interfering with the market for its products. The intelligent employer is also the one who recognizes that poor standards in any one industry, in the industries of the state, in the industries of the entire country, react upon the general competence of all labor; therefore raising standards of well-being generally will necessarily result in better and more efficient production.

In estimating the proportion, it may be of wages or of leisure or of expense in sanitary equipment that, as is commonly said, the trade will bear, it is usual to take into account three parties, the employer, the worker and the consumer. The consumer has to be studied, for if prices rise above what he can pay, or thinks he can pay, he economizes in some way or carries his purchasing power elsewhere. The consumer can also be educated up to intelligent buying and his sense of responsibility stimulated through the distribution of literature on standards, bad and good, of factory employment, of white lists and of union lists.

Besides these three parties to the industrial bargain, there is a fourth which includes them all, of which we all are members. That fourth party is termed, perhaps none too explicitly, the community or society. Upon the community all industrial wrongs and evils react; it may not be today, the penalty may be borne by a succeeding generation, but eventually it has to be paid. Further, if the community has to suffer in a weak and inferior citizenship, or in the undermining of the social structure, with the community also rests the hope of better things, the determination to embody in practice in the coming years nobler ideals.

When we apply these considerations to the question of legislation, especially for women, we begin to understand why it is that so much of our humane legislation has taken this form. Taking them all round, a large proportion of the women workers are young, even under age. Girls go into industry quite as young as boys, and they pass out of it, at least as regular workers, very much earlier. That so many young married women remain in industry, that so many older married women with children work for wages regular or intermittently, does not do away with the fact that the average age of the women workers, especially in factories, is at any given time notably lower than that of the men.

Girls proverbially have less chance of training; in their

earlier working years they are usually employed on any unskilled job they can get. This makes their work of less market value, for the employer can always get more girls, who in a few weeks will be the equals of those he loses, so that in the close competition for any job the girl has very little bargaining power. Girls and women of all ages are paid less for the same work. "Only a girl." "A very good wage for a girl." "She does good work for a woman." All these everyday phrases bear witness to the too common acceptance of a lower wage standard for the girl.

It is as a reaction from intolerable overwork, inadequate pay, underbidding by the underpaid, and the consequent utter waste of women's lives, that has come the movement toward the standardizing of women's work in the industries. It surely had been a better and a finer way, had it been possible, to secure honorable and self-respecting conditions of service through the organized power of the women workers themselves. In every trade strongly enough organized even locally, some such raising of standards has been the unfailing result of organization. What we win for ourselves we ever value more highly and hold more securely. But it would be inhuman to postpone the day of improvement until trade unionism among women becomes so general that they can act through the power of numbers. It is trade union women who have most ardently and efficiently championed the cause of their weaker sisters. Furthermore, it is the trade unions and trade union members, men and women alike, who have been most industrious in securing appropriations to enforce laws, in reporting violations and in seeing that laws are obeyed.

The arguments for legislation and against legislation have a singular monotony in whatever state the bills are introduced. The reasoning is of much the same complexion whether the subject of discussion be shorter hours, or pro-

INDUSTRIAL LEGISLATION

hibition of night work, or a minimum wage, except that in the latter case budgets come into consideration, and the price of a skirt and the cost of a meal and what allowance should be made to meet possible sickness or satisfy the human desire for recreation have to be gone into in considerable detail.

We will suppose that a familiar legislative hearing is on; the first objection always is that the trade cannot afford the cost of the reform; it will be such a loss to the employer that he would have to close up his business and go out of the state. It is to be noted that in spite of this oft-repeated and familiar threat there is not on record any single case in which an employer has been driven out of his state by any legislation whatever on behalf of his women employes. Not infrequently the much dreaded competition of another state free from such burdensome regulations has turned out on examination to be a veritable bogey. A manufacturer of woven cotton goods in a state which turns out only the finest cotton product will dramatically express his fear of the competition of his fellow manufacturer in a state turning out coarse cottons or even broad silks and ribbons. If limitation of hours is sought, the easy reply is that of course wages would be lowered, in spite of the invariable experience of every country, state or trade that has tried it, that earnings, possibly after some oscillations, inevitably adapt themselves to the new arrangement. A favorite plea is that the girls like to work long hours, and occasionally a poor overworked creature is dragged to a hearing to confirm her employer's contention. Or else the lawyer of a manufacturers' association, ready with many cunning devices and verbal quibbles which few employers would themselves stoop to use, will produce wonderful petitions from (of course unorganized) girls, expressing perfect contentment and satisfaction with things as they are. A favorite objection made by restaurant keepers, and in small towns, of storekeepers, to any disturbance of their arrangements is that the work is not continuous, that a girl can sit down when she likes, or that she has three hours off in the afternoon. Three hours off and no place to go, and no sense of being at leisure, for her evening's work is still ahead of her and perhaps a long car ride before she reaches her home in the late night hours.

Arguments in favor, too, are of one general trend, except that nowadays they strike an increasingly cheerful note. It is all the time becoming easier to prove that the state backward in this kind of legislation is more or less backward in other ways. The enormous bulk of evidence both in Europe and at home during the war showed by evidence not to be disputed that long hours and poor wages were not even productive of increased output, but notoriously lowered it. The principle of the short workday has been recognized by the United States Government and by more than half the states through the provision of an eight-hour day for the men in their employ. A development which could hardly have been foreseen forms nevertheless a very powerful reason why hours should be shortened by law. That is, that such a large proportion of employers, especially in large cities, are running their factories or keeping open their stores a far shorter time than the maximum permitted by law. In Illinois, for instance, although women may legally be asked to work 70 hours a week, the eight or nine hour day is the general rule in the principal industrial center, Chicago, and the Saturday afternoon holiday extremely common.

The modern discovery of the literally poisonous effect of over-fatigue upon the human system was first brought to the notice of the general public in this country by the

National Consumers' League through Josephine Goldmark and Louis D. Brandeis. The "toxin of fatigue" became a familiar phrase, and employers, lawyers, workers and social students were powerfully impressed by its dangers.

The arguments urged why conservation of health is most important in the case of women are two. The first is, that women are physically weaker and more readily injured by fatigue than men; the second and much the more convincing turns aside, as it were, from the individual woman and sees in her not merely the worker but the mother of the race, the creator of the next generation. This is an entirely new point of view. As a matter of public concern, the one striking fact that has stood out in all recent decisions by the courts on industrial legislation for women has been that it has upheld the police power of the state to make and enforce such laws as health measures, and as existing in the interest of the race. Said the Supreme Court, "as healthy mothers are essential to vigorous offspring the physical well-being of women becomes an object of public interest and care in order to preserve the strength and vigor of the race."

This is indeed an adapting to modern conditions of the long accepted idea that the feminine sex, as the transmitter and the guardian of life, requires protection as long as protection is possible from obvious and pressing danger. This is why women in a general way in pioneering days were not expected to undertake the roughest occupations or to face the risks of savage warfare. It is the reason today why in a shipwreck it is "woman and children first." The principle therefore comes down to us by honest inheritance, and is no mere gesture of an empty chivalry. When the continuance of the race is at stake this instinctive feeling will guard the woman and her offspring, or her offspring-to-be.

There has, however, been a long interregnum during which this sound creed was overlooked, at length forgotten, and allowed to slip into oblivion. It is so difficult for human beings to adapt their moral codes, or even their unconcious sense of the need of race preservation, to changed social conditions. The very man who would, to save a woman on board ship, yield her his place in the lifeboat and calmly step back himself to almost certain death, will today often fail to recognize, either as an employer, a fellow worker or a citizen, that machine industry is endangering the life and the health of women as much as could the overwhelming wave. The courts in reminding the community that its women citizens are the conservers of the race, have but translated the old phrase into a modern reading and set it up as a standard to be adhered to under modern conditions.

One indirect result of the limitation of hours is seen notably in the seasonal trades which employ so many women. As long as women and girls can be legally worked long hours the management tends to take all the orders it can get, to be executed within any time demanded, no matter how short the notice, with the natural consequence that orders presently slack off, and the girl, tired out after the rush season, but with no money to tide over a period of unemployment, is laid off to manage as best she may, either until she can place herself in some other job or until, with the oncoming of the busy season, her old trade calls for her again.

Behind and beneath all effort to pass an eight-hour law, to establish a minimum wage, or in any way to protect any workers, lies this high aim; the establishment either by the co-operative action of the workers or the intelligent and educated consent of the community, of such standards for industry as shall insure that the human beings, their personality and their possible abilities shall be considered of at least equal importance with the goods they turn out. Men in great numbers have striven to attain these ends through organization, but their efforts have been quite wisely and practically expressed through separate organizations and have been concentrated upon the freeing of separate groups, as the need of each group became more pressing, or its power to make those needs known grew. The piecemeal character of our legislation is quoted as a proof of inconsistency. It furnishes an equally good argument for the universality of the need of the legislation, no matter through what channel it can be obtained. Men have secured relief in groups and they will probably go on obtaining legislative relief in groups and for new groups.

Although men have in this country mostly depended upon organization to win improvement in their working standards, they have not hesitated to make use of legislation when that seemed the better plan. This is true for instance, of the federal employes. Every letter-carrier in the country enjoys an eight-hour day, by law. Most municipal workers, including the day laborer, work but eight hours a day. Men have been successful in obtaining legislation when the group was powerful enough and sufficiently unanimous and determined to obtain a hearing for their request. There seems to be no particular reason, therefore, why women cannot quite reasonably, and making no apology or excuse, ask that they be legislated for as a group, not necessarily as a sex.

The main difference regarding the woman worker is that on account of her many handicaps, youth, inexperience, poor training and poorer pay, she is rarely able to carry the whole burden of making the fight herself. She then very naturally accepts the aid of other women whose group interest and sympathy with her difficulties is awakened and keen.

Industrial legislation for women carries in its train sometimes a secondary result. Setting standards for women is setting a pace. The higher standards of cleanliness and conveniences of equipment that attract and keep women in a well-arranged factory, also set an example to the men workers, and when a new plant is opened men also reap the advantage. If an eight-hour law sends the women home at five or half-past five, it will not pay to run the power and keep the factory open for another hour or two just to make use of the factory's force of men, since in so many cases the hands of both men and women are needed in turning out a single finished article.

CHAPTER VIII

THE MINIMUM WAGE

Regulation of wages is now no new matter, but in former times regulation was directed toward preventing wages from rising too high, and there was no thought of fixing a minimum which should serve as a dyke against unregulated competition and so prevent the remuneration of the laborer from sinking too low.

The first effort in that direction was Samuel Whitbread's "Bill for Regulating the Wages of Labor," introduced into the House of Commons in 1795, when it was supported by Fox and opposed by the younger Pitt. At that time the old "combination laws" were in force forbidding any organization of the workers. The bill failed to pass, nor was any other legislation enacted to relieve the extreme poverty of that time. Starvation wages were supplemented out of the poor relief funds by magistrates, who, however they theorized against trade unions or against the raising of wages by law, were yet human and could not ignore the extremity of suffering which they saw before them.*

Just a hundred years later, in the young British colony of Victoria, Australia, there was observable increasing poverty in certain of the city trades. In 1895 some of the residents of Melbourne could no longer endure the situa-

---

* "The Village Labourer of 1760 to 1832," by Mr. and Mrs. J. L. Hammond, quoted by Edith Abbott in *Life and Labor*, January, 1915.

tion without protest. They formed an Anti-Sweating League, with Mr. Samuel Mauger as chairman. As a result of what the league unearthed, public opinion was thoroughly aroused, especially as to the revelations touching the lives led by poor sewing women working in their own homes.

Stories differ as to just how it happened that minimum wage laws and wage boards were proposed to the legislature. One tale runs that Mr. Alexander Peacock, the Chief Secretary, had been so impressed by New Zealand arbitration courts that he worked out this different plan. Another story has it that Mr. Peacock one day, in his own district of Castlemaine observed the gold miners at the head of the shaft, sitting over their mid-day meal in the open air of that mild climate discussing with the foreman a desired raise in wages. He went away with a new and challenging idea. If, he thought, one group of workmen can discuss wages with their employer's representative, why cannot all?

In 1896 minimum wage legislation was introduced. It was at first proposed to apply the law to women only. But finally it was made to cover all employes, of either sex, in the boot-making and baking trade, in most divisions of the sewing trades, and the furniture trade.

The act was temporary only, but it has been enacted and re-enacted, and always with increased scope, till in 1915 there were no fewer than 135 wage boards covering as many different trades; trades as varied as cigar makers, confectioners, saddlers, wood-workers, printers, photographers and even undertakers.

Up to 1914 many studies had been made of the Victorian wage-board plan, and it was fairly generally agreed that it had accomplished much of what it set out to do. Perhaps the legislation was not the cause of an increase in factories,

THE MINIMUM WAGE 145

but it at least had not prevented development. With its establishment were correlated shorter hours. Other trades, not covered, had not increased wages at the same rate and the workers in these trades still had to face the increased cost of living.

In accordance with the method of administration, if a request is made by a group of either employers or employes, it has to be brought before the legislature and if approved, the trade is brought under a wage board. The next step is the nomination of representatives by both employers and employes. These representatives select their own chairmen. The board thus constituted, is left to work out a decision, or as it is called, "a determination." It may take a long time and many meetings and much discussion to arrive at an agreement. When it has been reached, it is sent on to the Minister of Labor, becomes a part of the Factory Act, and is administered by factory inspectors. As Professor Hammond, who studied the whole matter on the spot, says, "Attention must once more be called to the fact that this whole system is merely a compulsory collective bargaining . . . I do not hesitate to say, however, that whether or not American employers or laborers like the wage-board plan, depends upon whether or not they favor collective bargaining."

The Arbitration Courts of New Zealand were established to prevent strikes; the wage boards of Victoria were planned to abolish sweating and to raise and standardize living conditions.

Since the beginning of the war in 1914 it has been difficult to draw inferences as to how minimum wage boards are functioning today, but according to latest account in the Commonwealth Year Book for 1918 minimum wage legislation has weathered the tremendous industrial shocks of the last seven years from which Australia in common with all other countries has suffered.

In Great Britain an agitation against sweated industries carried on by the Anti-Sweating Committee, followed up by a parliamentary inquiry, brought about in 1909 a law setting up trade boards, as they were called, in four of the worst paid trades, chain-making (by hand), machine-made lace curtain finishing, box making and . . . tailoring. Reports upon these trades, also prewar, show that wages were raised, in some instances as much as 100 per cent or more. Publicity was given to actual conditions, and thus the poorer employers were educated to learn from the experience of the more efficient, that high wages did not necessarily mean high cost.

The act was afterwards extended to include some other trades, such as the preserving of fruit and vegetables, candy-making, shirt-making, cotton embroidery and the making of hollow ware. A more startling application of the principle was to the coal miners in 1911 in an emergency measure after the coal strike of that year. The industrial crises which have come in the train of the war leave us without sufficient classified information on which to base an interpretation of the effect of wage regulation in Great Britain, as it stands today.

Mary Macarthur came from England in 1909 as delegate to the second biennial convention of the National Women's Trade Union League, and presented the case of minimum wage legislation in her own country. The Convention thereupon included in the League's legislative program "a legal minimum wage in sweated trades."

The Boston Women's Trade Union League took up the question. The co-operation of other organizations was secured. A bill was passed creating a commission of inquiry into the wages of women and minors, with the view of establishing wage boards. Its report resulted in the Massachusetts Act of 1912.

Mrs. Florence Kelley attended the International Conference of Consumers' Leagues in 1908, where the idea of standardized wages was put before her. Much impressed, she used her influence here, till it was made part of the platform of the National Consumers' League in 1910. In 1911 bills for minimum wage boards were introduced in three states, Minnesota, Massachusetts and Wisconsin. In Minnesota, through the Rev. John A. Ryan, a member of the minimum wage board committee of the National Consumers' League; in Wisconsin through the State Consumers' League.

In comparing American discussions on this subject and summing up American legislation, there are certain distinct differences to be noted in our own minimum wage laws, whether passed or only proposed, in this country, from those in operation elsewhere. In both Victoria and Great Britain, the object has been to abolish sweating and to set standards of wages for all employers. Men as well as women have been covered. In this country, owing to the peculiar rigidity of the United States Constitution, there have been many setbacks in the way of standardizing either hours or wages. "Freedom of contract" was successfully invoked in the Jacobs case (1885) to invalidate the New York state law forbidding the night work of women, and later on, in Illinois, under the Ritchie decision, the eight-hour law for women similarly came under the fatal ban of being unconstitutional.

When the advocates of industrial legislation took heart of grace once more, in the early years of the present century, they pursued a somewhat changed policy. Mr. Louis D. Brandeis placed the arguments for such legislation on a fresh basis; the law should be put in as a health measure, so important to the welfare of the community, that the police power of the state might be used to override the plea of supposed "freedom" of contract. The first test of the principle was made when Mr. Brandeis, as counsel for the National Consumers' League filed the brief prepared by Miss Josephine Goldmark and himself, showing the injurious effects of overwork, and especially its effects upon women as the potential mothers of the race. Ever since, this argument has had force with the state courts and with the Supreme Court of the United States whenever industrial legislation for women has been brought before them.

The arguments used then were afterwards elaborated and developed in a second brief and published later on in book form under the title "Fatigue and Efficiency" by Josephine Goldmark.

Massachusetts was the first state to pass a minimum wage law (1912). Unfortunately, as passed by the legislature, it carried no penalty, and the supporters of minimum wage legislation were greatly perturbed by this omission and hesitated as to whether they should accept the half loaf of law without a penalty, rather than the alternative of no law at all. All that could, or that can be done to bring rebellious employers to time is to publish a black list of their names, or, as a yet milder measure, a white list of those living up to the decree. Yet no one would deny that in spite of all its weaknesses, the Massachusetts law has raised standards in some of the worst paid trades, has educated the public to a better understanding of industrial matters, and has paved the way to minimum wage laws of a more effective type in other states. One result of such publicity was that the Progressive Party put the minimum wage for women in their national platform.

THE MINIMUM WAGE

In 1913 forty legislatures were in session, and the subject of regulation of wages for low-paid women was much discussed. In 1913–14 commissions were appointed to establish wage rates in California, Colorado, Minnesota, Nebraska, Oregon, Washington and Wisconsin, while there were commissions of inquiry in Connecticut, Illinois, Indiana and Ohio.

At date of writing, March, 1923, there are minimum wage laws for women in Arizona, Arkansas, California, Colorado, Kansas, Massachusetts, Minnesota, North Dakota, Oregon, Utah, Washington, Wisconsin and the District of Columbia.

One most significant decision was given in the Oregon test case, which, through a divided opinion in the Federal Supreme Court, left in force the favorable decision of the Oregon Supreme Court.

In defending the Oregon minimum wage law, Mr. Brandeis pointed out that no employer under it was compelled to employ any person, but the law did forbid his employing for wages a woman who receives less than a living wage, in the same way as other laws would prevent him from employing as an engineer someone who lacked the necessary training. In both cases, the public welfare was the primary consideration. He argued first, that low wages lead to both bad health and immorality. Second, that women need protection against being compelled to accept such low wages. Third, that adequate protection can be given only through such legislation.

There was an immense mass of evidence to show that poorly paid women either did not eat enough, or had wretched rooming arrangements, or were insufficiently clothed, or were helped out from improper sources. In no case could they lead a human life with a fair share of happiness, leisure and recreation. Leaving the woman herself out of the question, this condition of affairs was productive of a train of evils to the community.

In principle, there is nothing novel in such legislation; night work prohibition, limitation of hours, the safeguarding of machinery, these all affect the profits of the industry, or may do so.

The Massachusetts rate for candy workers in 1919 was $12.50. Other decrees, made in 1919 for experienced women workers, were the following:

District of Columbia, mercantile trade	$16.50
California, all women workers	13.50
Washington, all women workers	13.20
Massachusetts, candy occupation	12.50
Kansas, factories	11.00

The budget plan has been much in evidence, and how a woman may spend $4.00 a week in clothes and be respectably dressed is shown in the District of Columbia budget for women in the mercantile trades (1920).*

A great many advances have been made since the Massachusetts beginning; for instance, providing for increase of rates in proportion to increase in cost of living; fixing the value of meals and rooms furnished by employer in such trades as those of the waitress, so that board shall not be charged to the girl at any higher rate than breakfast 20 cents, lunch 25 cents, dinner 30 cents, and that these shall be bona fide meals.† The employer is not permitted to make any deduction on account of tips, which may or may not be received by the worker.

---

* Minimum Wage Commissions in 1920—National Consumers' League.

† These are the California rates.

THE MINIMUM WAGE

	Articles	Cost per year
3	Hats	$15.00
½	Coat	19.75
3 pair	Gloves	4.50
½	Suit	17.50
6	Waists	12.00
1	Wool skirt	10.00
½	Wool dress	10.00
2	Summer skirt	5.00
2	Wash dresses	16.00
1	Dress-up waist	5.50
½	Dress-up dress	14.75
4 pair	Shoes	31.50
..	Stockings	5.00
2 pair	Corsets	5.00
6	Corset covers	6.00
	Union suits:	
3	Winter	4.50
8	Summer	5.00
	Under skirts:	
1	Dark	3.95
2	White	3.00
1 doz.	Handkerchiefs	1.80
..	Neckwear	1.25
2	Aprons	2.00
½	Kimono	1.00
4	Night gowns	4.00
½	Umbrella	1.50
..	Rubbers	1.25
1	Purse	3.00
..	Repairing clothing	2.25
..	Repairing shoes	2.50
..	Miscellaneous	2.00
	Total	$216.50
	Less	8.50
		$208.00
	Total per week	$4.00

Sundries when separated into details make another illuminating page:

Items of classification employed by minimum wage commissions	District of Columbia Printing Trade Budget, April, 1919	Massachusetts Candy Trade Budget, June, 1919
	Per week	Per week
Car fare to and from work	$0.60	$0.76
Laundry	.75	.50
Medical care	.17*	.15*
Dentistry	.17*	.15*
Oculist	.16*	..
Religion	.05*	.11
Charity	.05*	....
Insurance	.18*	.15*
Savings	.17*	.15*
Labor organization	.05*	....
Magazines and newspapers	....	.18
Tuition (or self-improvement)	.10	.15
Stationery and postage‡	....	....
Vacation	.25	.40
Amusements	.20	.30
Social organization	.05*	....
Incidentals	.20	.25
Total	$3.15	$3.25

* When two items were lumped under one heading, as "Religion and Charity," the allowance is divided, and one-half entered under each heading.

‡ "Stationery and Postage," employed by six wage conferences, Washington, in 1914. Tables issued by Nat. Consumers' League.

THE MINIMUM WAGE

Nebraska was once on the list of states with a minimum wage law, although the law was never enforced. But when the laws of the state were codified, in 1919, the minimum wage law vanished into some mental waste basket. In Texas a minimum wage law was passed. But its opponents, finding that the women whom it would chiefly benefit were the exploited Mexican women who came across the border, succeeded in having it repealed. The legislature passed another and a very poor law. The Governor signed the repeal of the first law, but refused to sign the enactment of the second.

The Massachusetts law is at present under fire of criticism. Some of the manufacturers resented the fact that the award affecting their trade would, if obeyed, make a palpable increase in their payrolls, and having decided not to pay the minimum decreed did not mind their refusal being advertised. They therefore took advantage of a period of depression to attack industrial legislation.

Mrs. Dorothy W. Douglas in her careful analysis of "American Minimum Wage Laws at Work" (*American Economic Review*, December, 1919), speaks of "the inescapable fact" that of the fifteen states already having minimum wage laws upon their statute books only three have in operation rulings that are really satisfactory, all of the others being what she scathingly but truly terms substandard. We have a long road to travel yet before the "living wage" for all is an accomplished fact. Meanwhile every campaign for the standardizing of wages, every minimum wage law that is enforced helps in two ways, to bring home to the public the sense of responsibility for social conditions, and to encourage organization among the workers, and the working woman, has, after all, no such protection as that afforded by organization.

It will be news to most that minimum wage legislation

has during the last five years made rapid progress in Canada. The *Journal of Political Economy* for April 22 contains an article, the results of an investigation made by Kathleen Derry and Paul H. Douglas, which covers the ground thoroughly up to date. Five of the nine provinces of the Dominion, Alberta, British Columbia, Manitoba, Ontario and Saskatchewan, have minimum wage regulation. Two others, Nova Scotia and Quebec, have passed such laws, but they are as yet inoperative, leaving only New Brunswick and Prince Edward Island without such legislation. Among the causes given by the writers for this remarkable advance are these: the active support by the leaders of the Canadian labor movement; the absence of any constitutional difficulties and the comparatively weak position of business interests in Canada. The beginning was made in 1917 in the Province of Alberta when a clause in Factories Act provided that "No person shall be employed by an employer, in any factory, shop, office, or office building at a wage less than $1.50 per shift, except in case of apprentices who may be paid a wage of not less than $1 a shift." This did not prove satisfactory.

Minimum wage legislation did not really come into force in Alberta until after the provincial election of 1921, when the Farmer Labor party came into power; meanwhile minimum wage laws were passed in the other provinces named.

Among the most important characteristics of the Canadian legislation Mr. Douglas and Mrs. Derry mention the almost universal principle that the wages fixed shall be based on the necessary cost of living. They point out the nominal inclusion of men under the flat rate law of Alberta, and that the Miners' Minimum Wage Act of British Columbia opens a legal door to the possible governmental regulation of men's wages in Canada in the future, although there seems no present intention of including them.

Next, minimum wage boards and commissions in British Columbia, Manitoba, Nova Scotia and Saskatchewan have power over hours and conditions of labor as well as wages, while those of Ontario and Quebec have jurisdiction over wages alone. The experience of British Columbia and Ontario, however, indicates that it is impossible permanently to consider wages apart from the number of hours to be worked. There is a greater flexibility in making determinations according to locality and industry. The power of the boards themselves is very great. In the Quebec law power is given to the Minimum Wage Commission not only to reject or approve, but even to amend. So far as the experience goes of the only province, British Columbia, as to which there yet exist reliable data, the wages of the more poorly paid workers have been leveled up to a higher standard.

The laws in both Manitoba and British Columbia endeavor to cope with the problem of short time and irregular employment, not the fault of the worker. British Columbia, for instance, provides for those employed in places of amusement, higher hourly rates for those employed less than thirty-six hours, than for those employed more. In this connection the writers conclude:

It is highly desirable . . . that the principle of forcing employers to stabilize their production and lessen the irregularity of employment should be further developed and extended. Apparently the best method of dealing with this problem is that of the penalty differential wage for short time. Both Manitoba and British Columbia have at least pointed the way along which future progress should proceed.

Another observer reports Ontario as doing most and best work.

The minimum wage in this country has hitherto been

applied solely to women, with the idea of preventing the exploitation of a class of workers handicapped in many ways; but also because the health and welfare of women, as a class, is of even greater importance to society than that of men, inasmuch as the function of women as mothers, and potential mothers, is a more fundamental function than that of men as fathers. Upon the mother the child depends before birth, and for long years after birth for physical nurture, for personal growth. Although normally the father is the outside provider, and although he should and usually does share in imparting social training, for these reasons and because injury to the mother-sex is more hurtful to the future citizenship, have all these efforts been made for industrial legislation for women.

A word must nevertheless be said here, regarding a remarkable new development of wage standardization, applying to all workers with family responsibilities, and approaching the question from a totally different angle. This is known as the family wage, family allowances or endowment of motherhood, and is closely related to maternity insurance and mothers' pensions. In some countries it is a governmental or state affair; in others entirely or partly an arrangement carried out by large firms; or by whole industries. The essential principle is the payment to the worker or to the worker's wife, of a sum for the maintenance of the children, in proportion to the number in the family. In France 2,000,000 workers, chiefly employed in mining, the metal trades, transportation and the civil service, are at present in receipt of such payment. "In Germany," says Miss Mary Waggaman, October, 1921, in the *Monthly Labor Review* (U. S. Bureau of Labor Statistics), "there is a trend toward the regulation of wages and especially bonuses, in accordance with the worker's family responsibilities and not altogether in relation to his ability

THE MINIMUM WAGE

and output." She lists the Netherlands, Spain, Belgium, Czecho-Slovakia, Poland and Sweden as all inquiring and experimenting. The matter has been discussed under various forms in Great Britain, and was recently given great publicity in Australia through the appointment of a Basic Wage Commission.

The Commission had no power to make even a recommendation, and did not do so. Its report, however, asserted as proved that it cost in Australia on the average £5.16.0 ($28.13 at par value) a week to support decently a man, his wife, and three children under fourteen. The unions were satisfied; the employers declared they would be ruined, should legislation be carried through based upon such standards. The Commonwealth Statisticians, when consulted, reported that the entire income of the Commonwealth would not meet the bill. At the request of the Prime Minister, the Chairman of the Commission, writing as an individual, separated the basic wage into its constituent parts, and calculating that there was, on an average, barely one child to each male worker, proposed that each employer should pay his (unskilled) employes a minimum flat wage of £4.0.0 ($19.40) per week, whether single or married; the employer, in addition, to pay to the state as a tax the sum of a little less than eleven shillings ($2.58) for each unskilled male worker in his employ. The proceeds were to go into a pool. This pool, he calculated, would be sufficient to provide a child pension of twelve shillings ($2.88) for every child of the working class under fourteen. According to this plan, the man with a wife and three children could still look for £5.16.0, the man with two children less in proportion. Those with larger families, again, would have a larger income. This did away with part of the objection to the Commission's inflexible basic wage, that part of the money would be expended upon the "mythical children" of childless men.

The figures of the Chief Statistician and his inferences from them are equally disputed by trade unionists.

The sole actual result reported is that in December, 1920, it was announced that the married employes of the Federal Government were to be paid a basic wage, and, in addition, receive an allowance for each child.

The economic question is here seen reduced to its bare elements. The question raised cannot be answered without the production of facts. "What is the country's income?" "How can it be increased?" "How should it be distributed?" "What should be a first charge upon national income (net or gross)?" Work here, as suggested by Professor Heaton, for another Royal Commission.

Miss Eleanor Rathbone, describing a similar New South Wales State bill, "The Maintenance of Children," draws attention to an inequality between men and women wage-earners. Under this, if a wage-earning woman were supporting children, she would receive, as the head of the house, the same allotment for each child as if she were a man; but she would not draw the same individual wage as her husband would have done, although she is equally responsible for the family and family standards. On the other hand, a single man is supposed to need as much to spend on himself as he would spend on two, were he married and with no children.

Certainly one indirect result from systems of wage regulation is that the public becomes slowly educated to a knowledge of what manufactured articles cost, in terms of the life of the worker. The granting of fair wages becomes a matter of public concern and public responsibility.

Nothing in the nature of a child allowance has been tried

THE MINIMUM WAGE

in the United States, except in the form of mothers' pensions.

There is profound difference of opinion in economic and labor circles concerning this novel method of solving the wage problem; the few partial experiments in this direction are too recent for any definite conclusions to be arrived at. Many trade unionists regard such schemes with distrust, as confusing the issue between output and remuneration. Some advocates of birth control also point out that to insure the children's receiving full benefit, whether individually or through the raising of the standards of family life, either such family subsidy should be paid directly to the mother or she should at least have a legal control over its expenditure.

There is much industrial legislation which applies to men as well as to women; workmen's compensation; the long advocated health insurance and insurance against unemployment, also still in the future for the United States. The latter has been closely investigated by labor unions. The general opinion is more and more coming to be that in part, at least, it must be looked on as a charge on industry, to be foreseen, to be prepared for, and to be in part prevented. Contrary to the general impression, women suffer chronically from unemployment, partly owing to the seasonal character of so many of their occupations and partly because such a large proportion, particularly of the younger workers, are untrained or half trained, belonging to what are called the semi-skilled occupations, and therefore have not the hold upon a trade that is the valued possession of the skilled worker.

Anna Garlin Spencer, in "The Family and Its Members," warns us against linking together, as is so often done, adult women and children for legislative protection. She advocates as a social measure of the first importance minimum wage legislation or rather, perhaps, adequate wage standardization for fathers of families; adequate protection for the youth of both sexes, up to eighteen, including limitation of the working hours of the adolescent to an average of not more than 24 hours per week.

If we are as anxious as citizens to secure opportunity for the men and women who make up the great army of average workers, self-supporting but at cost of struggle often too severe, as we are anxious as philanthropists to ease the burden and protect the weakness of the more backward members of the industrial army, the current of upward movement of all in gainful occupations would be stronger and more socially helpful. The family is most of all concerned with the minimum wage of adult men who marry and have children. . . .

Social protection should be less a club marked, "Thou shalt not," and more an opportunity inscribed, "Chances to rise, win them." For the woman, married and a mother, there must be not so many new ways of enforcing prohibitions of what are deemed for her harmful forms of labor, as more ingenuity in providing half-time work, better adjustments of earning facilities to domestic duties, far more co-operative machinery for reducing the cost of living and for securing the family against economic exploitation in food, clothing and shelter.

The first women who asked for an investigation into the industrial condition of women and children appear to have had in mind woman and child workers in the broad and accurate meaning of all those who worked. The act under which the investigation was carried out read: "An Act to authorize the Secretary of Commerce and Labor to report upon the industrial, social, moral, educational and physical condition of woman and child workers in the United States." The interpretation put upon it, however, by the Department and everyone else was that the investigation was to concern itself with woman and child wage-earners.

THE MINIMUM WAGE 161

As it was, the task was so great that any other interpretation would at that time merely have meant either complete failure to achieve any result at all or an inadequate and superficial handling of the subject. No one, on the other hand, who is interested in an accurate interpretation of the meaning and value of woman's work in the community can be content to limit future inquiries to the wage-earning occupations.

The figures of the United States census are in this regard full of meaning. The census of 1920 lists, in round figures, 32,000,000 women over 16 years of age, of whom only 8,000,000 are listed as working, leaving about 24,000,000 to be accounted for. By working, the Bureau means working for wages or salaries or conducting businesses of their own. The rest of the 32,000,000, what are they doing? Under any non-technical interpretation, these women (and girls) are employed in caring for their families, in washing, cooking, sewing, cleaning, many of them incidentally having babies and bringing up these babies from infancy to full-grown manhood and womanhood. This is true even in cities; outside of cities the work of the home woman is still more arduous. It includes a great deal of real farm work both out of doors and indoors, besides the heavy burden of housekeeping for many of the farm workers.

Even while agreeing with Mrs. Charlotte Gilman that much of our domestic labor is ill planned and unprofitable, the fact remains that these women are producers, their labor contributing to the support of the nation and still more to the existence of the next generation; therefore to style the home woman as of no occupation is not common sense, for it does not fit in with facts. Furthermore, if statistics have any meaning, the number of those engaged forms an important element in comparing and valuing different kinds of work.

From our 32 million it will be necessary to make some deductions, for instance, women and girls of privilege and leisure and even idleness, a few; women owning their own businesses, not very many; girls between 16 and 20 still at school or college, a handful; and lastly the old and the frail, the sick and the permanently incapacitated; even after making all these deductions there must be well over 20,000,000 women left who are performing the everyday chores, taking care of the nation's homes and bringing up the nation's youth.

As a quantitative problem the twenty millions are even more important than the eight millions. It is true that the eight million wage-earning women have a social importance that the others yet lack. For one thing they can be found. They work in a sense in public or in the public eye. For the most part they do not work in isolation; for these reasons their work can be valued, estimated, judged. It can be interpreted from many different angles. The workers are themselves to a certain extent vocal. The worker learns to think and to be the cause of thought in others. In short, the wage earning occupations have come to be understood because they have been socialized. Out of the study of wage earning occupations, many of them conducted in behalf of women, we have learned a great deal of the effect of work upon the worker, of the stimulus given by higher wages or shorter hours; of the meaning of the seasonal trades, of the effect of unemployment on the health and psychology of the worker.

We may still be very ignorant of all these matters and the workers may still be sadly apathetic and only half awake to what is going on around them, but we have now learned a great deal and are in the way of learning more.

Very different it is with the home women, the twenty million home women. Yet they, too, have their economic

THE MINIMUM WAGE

and industrial and labor problems; they, too, have to face the problems of making ends meet; they, too, have to face the endless home struggle of finding enough to meet the constant demands for food, clothing and shelter.

The fact that the money part of the family income comes through the husband and perhaps through wage earning sons does not alter the fact that the value in expenditure of that income so largely depends upon the woman's contribution of her own individual labor and her own thought and care. Why not then follow out the very same lines of inquiry which have had such satisfactory results in the case of the wage earning woman?

A resolution was adopted by the last convention of the National Woman's Trade Union League (June, 1922) asking for a congressional investigation into the economic status and labor conditions of women in the home, both of the twenty million women working in their own homes and of the other two million women working for wages.

As this book is going through the press, there is a movement on foot, headed by no industrial group, but by a group of radical feminists, the National Woman's Party, to place upon a definite and formal basis, the demand that so many have believed to be implied in the demand for suffrage, and to be the necessary corollary of political emancipation, namely, that close on the heels of political equality, should follow legal and industrial equality. That may be asked for in the form of a federal amendment to the constitution, in the form of state amendments, or again it may be reached through piece by piece legislation, aimed at removing one by one, or group by group, such discriminations as bar women from jury service, from state or professional employment, from equality of parental rights. In some states the wife is today legally tied down to the domicile of her husband, even although she may be living in another state.

The great majority of such discriminations affect women through the sex relation, especially the marriage relation with its resultant economic dependence, but it is an error to suppose that the wage-earning woman and the poor woman is not a sufferer through these discriminations.

The objection raised against this campaign by most of the organized working women is that it would tend to abrogate legislation shortening hours and standardizing wages, by giving employers, lawyers and judges a loophole through which all such legislation for women might be declared unconstitutional. However that may be—state constitutions vary and lawyers differ radically in their forecasts of what may happen, a dynamic element enters into the case which cannot be passed over. It is with some astonishment that one observes women arguing for legislative action on the ground that such laws are needed as a concession to weakness, instead of being respected and valued as a means of raising standards in one field and for one group, just as by law, many other groups, miners, railway men and federal employes have had their standards raised year by year, without any sense in their case that it was a concession to weakness.

There is no question that this group of feminists are holding up a great ideal, and the psychological effect of such an ideal held steadily before women and before men must have in the end a profound influence upon thought and upon legislation. Some of its advocates take in addition, what seems to be the gratuitous step of being willing, for what they consider consistency, to scrap everything working women have with such toil and suffering obtained, in the raising of standards by legislation; taking the position that no such legislation should be passed to apply to women

THE MINIMUM WAGE

unless it is also extended to men. No such alternative seems either desirable or inevitable. Such a hard and fast rule is the less called for, inasmuch as many trade union men are not yet willing to ask for general limitation of hours for men, still holding to the position from which they have departed in Great Britain, that organization is the only channel through which men should obtain advance of hour or wage standards.

What will happen will largely depend upon the great mass of silent women themselves, and upon how keenly they are alive to the need of obtaining genuine economic independence and genuine equality. This mass of women recorded as not gainfully employed, may at length express their resentment at being discriminated against alike by law, through the administration of law, and through social customs and tradition.*

---

*In April, 1923, the United States Supreme Court declared the Minimum Wage Law of the District of Columbia unconstitutional. At time of writing, there exists extreme uncertainty as to what the ultimate results of this decision may be, and how far it may affect minimum wage laws which have been passed by the different state legislatures.

Chapter IX

THE WOMEN'S BUREAU

One most important development of the last ten years in the woman's labor movement has been the establishment of the Women's Bureau as an essential part of the Department of Labor. To know how this came about it will be necessary to go back a little into recent history. Although the need for such a bureau had long been felt, it is doubtful whether we should have had it today had it not been for the great changes in industry wrought by the World War.

For many years the sole way in which the public could come into connection with industrial questions was through the Department of Commerce and Labor, commerce being much the more important division and its activities emphasized accordingly. Mr. Charles P. Neill, who was Commissioner of the Bureau of Labor within the Department under the Roosevelt Administration is, however, to be remembered by working folks, because he took his responsibilities toward them very seriously.

In 1913 the Department of Commerce and Labor was formally divided, and the interests of labor handed over to the officials of the new Department of Labor. Mr. William B. Wilson, a miner, a man long an officer in his own organization, was made Secretary, and Mr. Louis F. Post, the well-known writer on public affairs, Assistant Secretary.

In the winter of 1905, the Illinois Women's Trade Union League, at one of its regular meetings, passed a resolution requesting the National League to appoint a committee to

THE WOMEN'S BUREAU

secure a federal investigation of the conditions of women in factories and shops. A committee of three was appointed, Mary E. McDowell chairman, with instructions to secure the co-operation of the General Federation of Women's Clubs and other organizations.

The committee visited Washington, and at once gained the support of President Roosevelt and the Commissioner of Labor, Mr. Charles P. Neill. Furthermore, they made the suggestion that the investigation should cover also the conditions of working children.

Representative Gardner of Massachusetts introduced the bill in March, 1906. It authorized the Secretary of Commerce and Labor to investigate and report upon the industrial, social, moral, educational and physical conditions of woman and child wage earners in the United States, allowing for an appropriation of $150,000.

The bill passed the following January (1907), but carried no appropriation. The right of the Federal Government to make such an investigation was questioned, but when that point had been favorably decided by the Judiciary Committee, the last obstacle had been passed, and the Commissioner was able to set to work, mapping out the scope of the investigation. The amount finally appropriated was $300,000.

The organizations that co-operated in securing the investigation were:

> American Federation of Labor, and International unions,
> State Federations of Labor,
> Brotherhood of Railroad Trainmen's Associations,
> General Federation of Women's Clubs,
> Daughters of the American Revolution, and Colonial Dames,
> Woman's Christian Temperance Union,
> Boards of Trade,
> Ministerial associations.

The special investigation lasted four years, issuing reports at intervals, and covered much ground, as can be judged from some of the titles: "The Silk Industry," "The Glass Industry," "Labor Laws and Factory Conditions," "Family Budgets," "Women in Trade Unions." When in 1911 the report was complete, it filled nineteen volumes. It is to be found in all important libraries. It laid a sound foundation of knowledge in a field where public ignorance had been dense and public interest, except in a few quarters, lacking.

The report made a profound impression, and what was unveiled regarding wages, sanitary conditions, the health of the workers, the erratic and inconsistent standards prevailing in wages and hours, the prevalence of seasonal work and consequent unemployment in so many women's trades, was found to be so much worse than could have been imagined that labor leaders and social workers who had previously seen below the surface for themselves, had now plenty of proof, and more than plenty, to confirm their fears and to support their gloomiest words of warning. With all this information in hand, it soon became evident that what was needed was not an occasional investigation, monumental as this one had been, but a permanent office with officials always on the job. It was not long before an organized movement was on foot among the women of the country, making a definite request for the establishment of a Women's Division in the Department of Labor for the handling of women's industrial problems.

Meanwhile the Children's Bureau had been established as a division of the Department of Commerce and Labor and had proved an astonishing success and a constant surprise to the legislative and departmental heads of Washington. Incidentally, it turned out to be a most powerful argument for the establishment of a Women's Bureau. The courage and independence of its head, Miss Julia Lathrop, and her keen sense of the close relation between industry and general well being, between the remuneration of the wage earner and the health and even the life of his babies, gave fresh courage to the advocates of a women's division, and they were more persistent than ever in urging that something similar to what had been done for the children of the nation was badly needed by the women workers.

In Manchester, New Hampshire, the Children's Bureau found that "of the babies with fathers earning less than $450 a year, about one in four died before it was twelve months old. The great majority of the babies had fathers in the wage group from $450 to $849, and of these about one in six died. Of the babies whose fathers earned $850, but less than $1,050, one in eight. This is exactly half of the infant deaths in the poorer families.

Again, in 1918, the Chief of the Bureau, in her annual report, summarized information secured in eight cities, Johnstown, Pa., Manchester, N. H., Brockton, Mass., Saginaw, Mich., New Bedford, Mass., Waterbury, Conn., Akron, Ohio, and Baltimore, Md. Taking an average of the whole where the father earned under $450, more than one baby in every six died; where the father earned $1,250 and over only about one in sixteen died.

In one of its early reports, the Children's Bureau had shown that of the approximately 15,000 deaths of women from childbirth occurring in the United States yearly, a large proportion is quite preventable. This heavy death rate occurs principally among the poor, where the attention the mother receives is that of the Middle Ages. Comparatively few mothers die where the family can afford twentieth century medical and nursing care.

The response to the women's insistent demands came

when the Women's Division was at length inaugurated in Washington. It was, however, but a subdivision of the Bureau of Labor Statistics. It had no independent head, no power of initiative, nor its own purse. The Chief was Miss Marie Obenauer. She had her seat as one of the five executives of the Bureau. She was, however, but one woman, and her co-officers were four men. In any difference of opinion where the interests of women were concerned, she would almost inevitably be outvoted. She had, it is true, a strong personality, and she was notably ingenious in securing the cooperation of State Bureaus of Labor. In Indiana she directed an investigation, the expenses of which were met by the Indiana State Bureau. In Washington, in the same fashion, she made a study of minimum wage-rates. She was successful in obtaining widespread publicity for her Division, and for a long while no one outside of Washington realized that, after all, it was a losing fight in which she was engaged. After a time Miss Obenauer resigned, and Miss Cunnington took her place, but she remained only about six months.

One of the wits of *The New Republic* contributed to the joy of readers by an airy account of how the Division functioned in industry, how it made for efficiency, and was helpful both to manufacturer and to employe and how, alas! it died of too much red tape and too little money.

"Show her in," said the manufacturer ungraciously. It was another of those impractical pests, an investigator.

"I have been studying factories equipped with your machinery," began the unwelcome guest, "and it struck me that some slight alteration would do away with a good deal of unnecessary strain upon the workers." Off came her gloves and out came her notebook and pencil.

"Those foot treadles, for instance; the range is 12 inches, and they require 100 pounds pressure to operate. Now when a woman steps up 12 inches and presses down a hundred pounds' weight all day long, she is working under a ruinous strain. Why not make the casting with a shorter range—thus—and install it thus, so that she steps down on it?"

The practical manufacturer looked at her penciled diagram, then he looked shrewdly at her.

"Where do you come from, anyway?" he asked abruptly.

The impractical one pulled out her credentials. They revealed the imposing title of Chief of the Women's Division of the Bureau of Labor Statistics of the United States Department of Labor.

"Well," said the man, with a grin, "I give up! What you suggest is perfectly practical. We never thought of it, that's all. We manufacturers have a right to be afraid of you people; usually you throw rocks at us and don't tell us what to do!"

In half an hour they had figured out schemes for relieving the heat with asbestos deflectors and a dozen other simple, practical improvements. Then the manufacturer got excited over a plan for getting perfected machinery standardized by the O. K. of the Federal Government and having the manufacturer share liability with the employer where unapproved machinery is used.

At this interesting point the investigator withdrew because Uncle Sam decided he did not have enough money to waste on allowing her to finish; the manufacturer is still trying to get her back.

Quite evidently, fresh legislation was needed. Secretary Wilson was entirely favorable to the re-organization of the Women's Section as a separate Division, and in 1916, the Jones-Casey bill was introduced into both houses, providing for the establishment in the Department of Labor of a Women's Division, "which shall investigate and report to the said department upon all matters pertaining to the welfare of wage-earning women, and shall especially investigate the questions of the competitive influence of women in the several industries, the adjustment of modern industrial mechanism and management to the physical and nervous organization of women, and the influence of industrial employment upon the subsequent home life of wage-earning women." The bill was backed by the National Women's Trade Union League, the National Consumers' League, the General Federation of Women's Clubs and the National Young Women's Christian Association and bore the recommendation of the Secretary of Labor.

With the introduction of this bill began a long weary effort to insure its passage. The struggle began in the spring of 1916 and cannot be said to have ended until the Women's Bureau was finally placed upon a permanent basis in June, 1920.

Meantime, the stars in their courses were fighting for Sisera and here there is a digression. During the early years of the World War, and before America entered it, it had already been abundantly shown that huge disorder and untold suffering resulted from throwing workers, especially women, in great numbers into new employment, where any old building had been turned into a factory overnight, where little provision had been made for the commonest needs of human beings, if they were to be kept clean and healthy, and ordinarily comfortable at their work, where perhaps neither housing, nor the means of daily transportation between home and factory had been considered.

If there was confusion and inadequacy in the material make-up of factory buildings, and in the local surroundings, there was apt to be even greater bewilderment over the allotting of jobs, the placing of workers, and the shifting of workers from one state or city to another. Result, that the workers were not to be had where they were needed, and the workers seeking jobs did not know where to find them.

Upon working women especially, usually the invisible

THE WOMEN'S BUREAU

partners in the industry of our country, quite a bright light was thrown, when, immediately war was declared, they were mobilized in a volunteer army, and called upon to march forward to fill gaps left in industry by the departing soldiers, and to fill likewise many new niches in the war trades, which without their aid, would have been crying out for help.

To remedy the evils that were piling up along with the increasing employment of inexperienced workers in the war trades, the Industrial Service Section of the Ordnance Department in Washington was established with Dean Schneider at the head and Miss Mary Van Kleeck as head of the Women's Section. While production, economy and efficiency were the immediate objects they were not the sole aim. Conserving the strength of the workers (particularly the women workers), and therefore the strength of the nation, was equally important. To adjust the two meant a great deal of planning; it meant talking over difficulties and patiently trying to harmonize the needs of the department as to output with the claims of the workers as to what they felt to be a living wage, endurable working hours, and decent housing arrangements.

Mary Van Kleeck had been director of the Committee on Women's Work and of Industrial Studies under the Russell Sage Foundation. Her chief duty now was to maintain a constant oversight over the girls turning out ordnance supplies (mainly, but not entirely munitions) in the various arsenals.

To do all this she had to keep in closest touch with the employes. She had to go outside of her office, and personally or through her corps of women aides, find out how the girls were getting on. Were they satisfied, and if not, why not? Were they giving satisfaction, and if not, why not? Usually there was some central question around which discontent or complaint centered, and it was not necessarily the same in different establishments. A superintendent might emphatically and sincerely believe that he could not possibly manage without overtime, and yet the trained adviser might discover that, after all, some rearrangement of work or of operators, or some better shop equipment might remove the necessity for long hours on that order. Sometimes a foreman who can manage men is quite unsuited to handle girls. Or the source of difficulty might lie outside the arsenal walls altogether, in crowded rooms, poor food, or a town trolley system so inadequate to accommodate the girls on their daily journeys night and morning that they come to work tired and inefficient, or make a bad record for attendance. The girl who utters no complaint to her superior, because she dare not, or thinks she dare not, but simply leaves, is a very usual type, and to her Miss Van Kleeck's helpers used to make the approach, used to link up with her, and find out why she left. Perhaps it had been for some perfectly good reason, but the cause of her dissatisfaction might be removable. Anyhow, whatever it was they would do their best to find it out. And it is wonderful how many causes of complaint can be done away with, if there is somebody with whom to talk things over, especially when there is such a very human sort of person holding the reins, someone who will not jerk the reins, just hold them steady.

Miss Van Kleeck appointed as her field assistant Miss Mary Anderson, well fitted on account of her long experience as a worker, as a member of the National Executive Board of the Boot and Shoe Workers' Union and also as an organizer for the Chicago and the National Women's Trade Union League. Her talent for getting at the heart of a matter had often helped in clearing away difficulties and settling shop disputes.

THE WOMEN'S BUREAU

Though the wage story here, and length of hours there, and in yet another case a place to live was the problem, and this girl or that forelady or that section boss wanted the trouble righted, it was in the office of Dean Schneider and his woman assistant administrator that plans were formed, and the principles laid down which enabled a peacemaker's decision to be accepted by the often irritated disputants in the shop. The Industrial Service Section was essentially a clearing house, in which every one's complaints, whether settled or still in the balance, eventually drifted. This was how the experience of one arsenal helped another instead of it being a case of hit or miss with each fresh trouble.

All this time women in every part of the country were pressing for a Women's Bureau. At length as an emergency measure room was made at Washington for the Woman in Industry Service in the Department of Labor. Miss Van Kleeck and Miss Anderson were transferred from the Ordnance Department to take charge as director and assistant director. Although the Woman in Industry Service never had any power to compel anybody to do anything, it did provide a forum for discussion and consultation, and was able to do an important educational work in preventing hysterical campaigns to overthrow such protective safeguards over women's hours and women's health, as long years of effort had established. Also, even with the tiny appropriation of $40,000 to cover everything, salaries, office and traveling expenses, and fees for aid of expert assistants, it was possible to answer many other calls for information, advice and help, calls that came from other government departments, from private employers, and from the working women themselves.

One of the very best pieces of work done was the inquiry into the chemical industries of Niagara Falls, N. Y. It arose out of the request of the local Employers' Association to be permitted to work women at night, thus overriding the New York state law. It was found that so many changes would have been necessary to insure reasonably healthful conditions for women that it was not possible to recommend their employment in these factories at that time. But better still was the making clear how many improvements could and should be installed immediately to make the work safe for the staff of men already engaged there, such as using mechanical devices for pulling and hauling of heavy weights, removing poisonous dusts and fumes from the air breathed by the employes, and strengthening the resistance of the individual through medical supervision and shorter hours of work.

There is a story told of one business man, who, during the war, hied him to Washington to procure a permit to have some women workers put on a night shift. The only consolation he received was "All these cases have to be passed upon by the Woman in Industry Service, and you'd never get by them. Better go back home and manage the best you can!" Which discreet advice was duly taken.

The fact that a few exceptionally skilled or specially trained women drew large pay in munition plants gave rise to the popular illusion that women's wages had been permanently raised all round. The Woman in Industry Service found little evidence to support this idea. Wages in the candy trade, for instance, had before the war been very poor. After the armistice was signed, inquiries were made in Philadelphia, and it was found that the wages were still so low that they had not nearly caught up with the increased cost of living. Besides this, candy making is so irregular a trade that days and weeks out of work are not uncommon. While there is then no money coming in, food and rent have to be met just the same; clothes have an unhappy knack of wearing out, and a doctor's bill to be met either for the girl herself or for someone belonging to her is always a dreaded possibility.

Who would think of such a trifling article of wear as garters implying waste of child life, the spread of infectious illness, and wretchedly low wages paid for the work of mothers in their own homes? And yet that was what was found in Bridgeport, Connecticut—typical, doubtless, of what exists in many lesser Bridgeports.

It has been said that of all the hard fates to be met, the very hardest that the American-born child can face is to be born a little colored girl baby. And this sad truth is here put in words that may be reserved in expression, but contain depths of suffering for our colored sisters. Representatives of the Woman in Industry Service, on one trip, visited 156 establishments in the Middle West, employing over 16,000 Negro women and it is written thus: "General standards for this class of workers were found to be decidedly more restricted than those of other women workers!" "Lower than the average!" and that is low enough. "Industrial opportunities decidedly more restricted!" and how restricted these are even for the white girl, only the working woman knows.

On Monday, November 11th, 1918, the very day the Armistice was signed, Miss Van Kleeck submitted to the Chairman of the War Labor Policies Board a note, urging that women be recognized as in industry to stay. Shortly afterwards the Woman in Industry Service issued what was perhaps its most far-reaching and important bulletin. This was a small pamphlet entitled "Standards for the Employment of Women in Industry" and was a statement in concise and compact form of the hours, wages and working conditions which were recommended for the employment of women in industry. These standards established practically a "code" for women in industry and offered a program which was welcomed by all those who were working to improve conditions.

The standards had been drawn up with the advice of both employers and workers, and before they were published had received the endorsement of many representative organizations. The pamphlet had an immediate and most phenomenal success, and has been used extensively throughout the country, being now in its third edition, more than one hundred and ten thousand having been distributed to individuals upon their request. In these standards among the points specially dwelt upon was the need of equal pay for equal work, women also to receive whatever proportionate increases men received. Great stress was laid upon the importance of workers sharing in the responsibility for industrial conditions. Responsibility can be placed, however, only through some form of organization, or, as the report puts it, "The genuine co-operation essential to production can be secured only if definite channels of communication between employers and groups of employes are established."

In August, 1919, Miss Van Kleeck retired and Miss Mary Anderson was appointed her successor. The Woman in Industry Service was guaranteed temporary existence as a holdover, but its future was most precarious, as long as it was only an emergency institution to meet the demands of war times or even of the reconstruction period. The women's organizations therefore redoubled their efforts to put the Woman in Industry Service upon a permanent basis.

After a long struggle, and many disheartening set-backs, the Kenyon-Campbell bill was finally passed in June, 1920. This established a Women's Bureau in the Department of Labor to "formulate standards and policies which shall promote the welfare of wage-earning women, improve their

THE WOMEN'S BUREAU

working conditions, and advance their opportunities for profitable employment." The Bureau naturally took over the organization and the staff of the Woman in Industry Service, and when it started as a Bureau, had already to its credit a mass of information and reports.

These reports covered such subjects as:

"The Employment of Women in the Government Service." This report disclosed the fact that women were not allowed to take Civil Service examinations for a large proportion of the positions in the Government service, and that the prevailing entrance salaries paid to women were much lower than those paid to men. As soon as this information was brought to the attention of the Civil Service Commission all examinations were opened to both men and women.

"Industrial Training for Women and Girls"—a survey of opportunities in industry and the vocational training available for women.

"The Effect of Laws Regulating the Employment of Women in Industry." Two studies had been made of this subject, one showing methods of employing women as street car conductors and ticket agents under different legal regulations, the other showing changes in the employment of women in the electrical and rubber industries in two states, one of which had recently established a 48 hour week for women while the other permitted a 60 hour week.

Investigations had been made of labor conditions for women in Indiana, of the possible employment of women during the war in the chemical industry in Niagara Falls, of the wages of women candy workers in Philadelphia, and of home workers in Bridgeport, Connecticut.

Summaries of all laws affecting women in industry had been prepared in chart and pamphlet form; exhibit material in the form of colored maps illustrating the status of the different states in regard to legislation for women, and posters illustrating standards for the employment of women in industry, were in circulation, and the Woman in Industry Service in the two years of its existence had become known over a large territory as a consulting and policy forming agency which could give valuable information regarding the problems of the employment of women in industry.

During the two years since the establishment of the Women's Bureau similar work has been carried on until, to glance over what has been accomplished up to the beginning of 1923, is indeed to cover a wide field.

A number of state investigations have been carried out and in time doubtless we shall know something of the conditions under which wage earning women work in every state in the Union. If there is one lesson more than another that has been driven home to us through these inquiries it is the need for common legislation, and the only legislation which can include residents of every state is federal legislation. We see this illustrated in graphic fashion in the colored charts issued by the Bureau. Look over a series of maps tinted in a regular checkerboard fashion in a variety of patterns according to whether it is a picture of women's daily legal working hours or of their weekly hours, or a chart of how long they may work at night, or in which states there are wage laws. You will be dazed and bewildered, and touched with a sense of the feebleness and futility of it all. Nature turns us out physically pretty much on the same model and if the women in Massachusetts or Minnesota or Oregon need to have their wage standardized then their sisters in Pennsylvania or West Virginia or Texas need it just as much. Here is what is happening in Virginia:

A typical story of the life of a working woman whose hours are from 7.30 a.m. to 6 p.m. was told to one of the investigators by the woman herself. Deserted by her husband and with two little children to support, she went to work in a tobacco factory. To be at the factory at 7.30 she had to get up at 5.30, cook breakfast, dress the children and take them to a day nursery, leaving home at 6.30. As the factory did not close until six in the evening she had to stop for the children on the way home, and did not get home until 7 o'clock. Then the housework must be done, and the children's clothes made, with the result that bedtime did not come much before midnight. This is not a story of an isolated case. Fifty-nine women were interviewed by the investigators and 37 of them supported others than themselves, 21 being responsible for the care and maintenance of children. The women who were interviewed were selected entirely by chance, as they were met in the factory, in the Y.W.C.A., at the day nurseries, or in their homes, so they can be considered to be fairly representative of the entire group of working women who were included in the survey.

So much for long hours. As to night work, comparatively few women in Virginia were found working at night, still a mere trifle of over seven hundred women were employed by establishments operating night shifts. The moral drawn by the Bureau is that it might be well to check night work before it becomes a common practice.

The particular hardship to women of employment during the night hours, which has been emphasized many times in different reports and investigations, was brought out again by the Women's Bureau investigators in stories of several women who worked at night in a tobacco factory in one city in the state.

Mrs. ——— was waiting at 7 p.m. to see if she could get a job on the night shift. Her husband was living and working, but she had been sick ever since her baby came, about three months ago, and they had gotten into debt. She couldn't leave the baby day times, but her husband could look out for him at night. She had worked in the factory before the baby came, almost up to the time he was born, but had "pleurisy and fever" ever since. Doctor didn't want her to go to work but she felt she must.

Mrs. ———— did day work during the summer but did not like it because it kept her away from the children. She has two children, one 5 and one 4 years old, and another coming in a couple of months. Her husband works in another state and sends money home, but not enough. By working at night she can be with the children and do the housework in the daytime. She sleeps a couple of hours in the morning and a couple in the afternoon. Her sister-in-law stays with the children at night.

Surely it is in the interest of the state to see that such sacrifices as these shall not be required or permitted. Under the strain of this double work women are unable to give either family or industry the attention and interest which are needed by both.

There is, however, another moral to be drawn and that is that the chief evil of long hours or of night work is the fact that the longer hours women work and the more they are engaged in night work, the more surely are they women carrying on two jobs. Two jobs mean the sapping of efficiency, ruin to health, the absence of all social or family life, disaster to childhood and utter misery to the unfortunate mother herself. Worse still is home work. For an illustration of this, let us go to Bridgeport, Connecticut, where pregnant women were found working on footpower machines, and carrying heavy packages of work to and from the factory. One such poor woman used to draw a little express cart a distance of two miles to save carfare, and then carried her bundle up three flights of stairs. A little girl of nine in another home was operating a footpress used in finishing garters. When asked "When do you have time for play?" her answer was "Sometimes on Sunday!"

THE WOMEN'S BUREAU

Principally through the extensive organization of the clothing trade, home work has been abolished to a great extent in the larger centers, but when we go outside of these centers, into smaller cities in many of the smaller trades, the Bureau has found home work in full swing. Home work is a combination of every possible evil. It means endless hours, night work, insanitary conditions, neglect and overwork of children. It means irregular and incredibly low wages and the carrying by the worker of a large part of the overhead expense of the manufacturer. Why should the worker, asks the Bureau, supply housing, heating, lighting, equipment and frequently machinery? Therefore, the Director recommends that home work be gradually eliminated after steps have been taken to prevent hardship in individual families.

It is interesting to note that in most of the recommendations the Bureau emphasizes the point that the standards of limitations of hours, home work and sanitation should not be considered as applying *only* to women, for men, too, are the victims of industrial pressure, but as applying *especially* to women because of their double function as wage earners and as mothers, and any injury they suffer is inevitably passed on, directly or indirectly, to the next generation.

More and more is the Bureau invading that stronghold of industrial poverty, the Solid South. It is gratifying to know that this is being done at the request and with the co-operation of the finest and most patriotic citizens of the southern states, both men and women. A special report upon Negro women in industry has just been published.

Most interesting is the publicity put out by the Bureau. Besides special reports and annual reports, there is a news service and more popular than any is a two-reel motion picture film, illustrating standards for the employment of women in industry, entitled "When Women Work." The film is lent free of charge to organizations who satisfy the Bureau that they will put it to good use, all expenses of transportation and showing being met by the borrowers. During the first year the film was released, beginning December, 1920, it was shown by 67 organizations in 26 States and the District of Columbia.

The value of the Bureau's work is seen in other directions. Not only are there repeated requests for special articles on different subjects pertaining to women in industry, but members of the staff are frequently called in for consultation by employers and others who wish information on methods of improving conditions. One manufacturer whose plant was visited during the course of one of the state investigations made by the Bureau, asked that its representatives assist him in making plans for standards and equipment in a new plant which he was planning to open.

Other studies which have been made by the Bureau include a detailed analysis of the material which can be obtained from the Census schedules, showing the social importance of much of the information which appears on Census schedules, but which the Bureau of the Census, because of lack of appropriation, has been unable to compile. A study has been made of the changes in the occupational status of women as shown by comparing the figures in the census reports for 1910 and 1920. The investigators have also turned to the records of the United States Patent Office, and a report has been prepared showing the great number and scope of inventions which have been patented by women during the past ten years.

The United States, however, will not be able to make full use of the Bureau until there is in every state a corresponding women's bureau in the state department of labor. As we have seen, the Federal Women's Bureau has no power of administration. Strictly speaking, it has no laws to administer. Labor laws are state laws, and their enforcement is a state function. The work of the Women's Bureau in investigating, in advising legislation, and furnishing information to state departments, and in educating public opinion up to demanding high and uniform standards in industry, can become effective only as the states are equipped with the machinery to make it effective. An indispensable part of such machinery is the state women's bureau.

At present there are but four states meeting in whole and five states meeting in part this requirement. Minnesota heads the list with its Bureau of Women and Children established in 1913 and now under the State Industrial Commission. Wisconsin has under its Industrial Commission a Woman's Department. New York in 1919 established the Women's Bureau in the State Department of Labor. But the measure establishing it provided no funds for its support. Accordingly for the first year of its existence its cost was met from a private fund, raised by the civic spirited women citizens of the State. Indiana has a Department of Women and Children in the Industrial Board.

In the five States of Washington, Oregon, California, Kansas, and Massachusetts, although there is no separate bureau or division for the interests of women, there is a woman member on the Industrial Commission who has a certain amount of authority.

Chapter X

WORKING WOMEN AND THE WAR

During the universal confusion attendant upon the declaration of war by so many European nations simultaneously, there was very great ignorance as to the industrial situation in the countries actually engaged, and hardly less ignorance as to what was taking place among ourselves as the indirect result of the happenings on the other side of the Atlantic. To take the European situation first, and Great Britain as typical of Europe, what happened was this: War had come overnight. Industry was dislocated. Men were enlisting on all sides. A sudden strain was put upon all those trades which manufactured anything that could conceivably be used in war, or for the support of the army. Strange to say, the first effect upon the women workers was a scarcity of employment, for the larger number of women had been engaged in producing not the basic necessities of life, but largely superfluities, such as fancy goods and articles of adornment, and the demand for these immediately fell off. The resulting slowing down of industry, while hard to meet, proved to be a temporary condition, and before long there was a call for women to enter every other kind of occupation, manufacturers as a whole being overwhelmed with orders. As the universal impression was that the war would soon be over, there was no limit to the hours worked, either by the men who were left or by the women newly drawn in. Night work and Sunday work became the rule in many factories

WORKING WOMEN AND THE WAR

and the trade unions saw the results of more than half a century's effort swept away. At the end of the first year, dissatisfaction was widespread. The production of war supplies was inadequate to meet military needs, and at the same time the workers were discontented and rebellious. The Government appointed a committee to look into the health of the munition workers. The investigators made remarkable discoveries and prescribed drastic remedies. They recommended for adult males a maximum working week of 65 hours with a rest of one day in seven; for women, not over 60 hours, and advised that the factories should provide proper arrangements for eating, suitable sanitary equipment with doctors and nurses in attendance to treat accidents, and should also take all possible precautions against industrial poisoning. The results were as startling as they had been unexpected. One example given was that of a group of men on very heavy work who had their hours reduced from 61 to 55 and who yet increased their total output by ten per cent.

The committee found that even paying overtime was a poor remedy for the evil of continuous seven day work. As one foreman tersely put it: "Sunday work gives six days' output for seven days' work for eight days' pay." The committee went on "except for short periods, continuous work (*i.e.*, the seven day week) is a profound mistake and does not pay. Output is not increased, . . . the munition workers in general have been allowed to reach a state of reduced efficiency and lowered health, which might have been avoided without reduction of output by attention to the details of daily and weekly rest."

Very much the same reactions were observed in the war-stimulated industries of this country. The minds of Americans were even more confused on account of our distance from the scene of conflict, the vast extent of territory and the division of the industrial sections among so many different states, each one with its own labor laws, and no common policy. It was not long before organized labor, social workers and women leaders discovered the evil tendencies that were at work and the disastrous results to our young womanhood of the high pressure under which they were being compelled to work.

The investigations made by Miss Amy Hewes, Professor of Economics at Mount Holyoke College, in 1916, for the Russell Sage Foundation, showed that in the munition plants of Bridgeport, "the new world arsenal," increasing speed of production was lengthening daily hours and imposing night work upon women, while the rapid growth of a boom town created congestion and confusion in living conditions for the large number of men and women workers who were crowding into the city to meet the new demands for labor. Dr. Alice Hamilton, now assistant professor of Industrial Diseases at Harvard, covered ten states in her investigation into health conditions in munition plants for the United States Bureau of Labor Statistics, and she found in many of them the grossest neglect of common cleanliness, buildings hurriedly thrown up, no washing facilities to get rid even of the poisonous dust, nor medical care to prevent sickness. The installation of exhaust systems for carrying off fumes and dust was postponed because they could wait while the machinery for production could not. "There is no way of knowing," she says, "how much illness and death resulted from this mad rush to get out explosives in a shorter time than they could properly be made."

There was the threat from every quarter of the wholesale abrogation of legal protections so slowly gained. The United States Navy Yard went on a ten-hour basis, the first breakdown of the eight-hour law for federal employes. In the New York Legislature the fight was on for more than a year to throw the entire labor code (even including the child labor law) upon the scrap heap. From many groups elsewhere came the demand for the total or partial abolition of all restriction upon hours. The Governor of Vermont approved an Act, empowering the authorities to suspend existing laws relating to the employment of women and children, while the United States was at war. In New York similar action was taken, but was vetoed by the Governor of that State.

The advantages of long years of co-operation between the groups standing for humane conditions in industry were seen when in opposition to the demand, a demand in some quarters coldly intentional, in others merely with a foolish and hysterical motive, all these large organizations came out in united protest, saying that it was for those who wished labor laws abolished to show cause why this should be done. The principal bodies were the American Federation of Labor and many of its internationals, the National Women's Trade Union League, the Consumers' League, the American Association for Labor Legislation, the National Child Labor Committee, the National American Woman Suffrage Association and the National Young Women's Christian Association. Their position was strengthened by the information, by this time made public, regarding Great Britain's experience and how she had had to retrace her steps. They were backed by the statements of the United States Department of Labor, emphasized by the reports of Miss Julia Lathrop of the Children's Bureau. Moreover, many of the largest employing firms and of the best employers were emphatic in urging caution. Mr. Redfield, Secretary of Commerce, cited the experience of his own firm, the J. H. Williams Company of Brooklyn, N. Y., as an example of the wisdom and economy of short hours. Others who gave evidence of the business advantages of the eight-hour day over either a ten or a twelve hour day were the Commonwealth Steel Company, the Solvay Process Company of Syracuse, N. Y., Mr. Thurston Ballard of Louisville, Ky., the Ford Company, the Studebaker Company, the McElwain Shoe Company, and the Endicott and Johnson Shoe Company with many other large firms. Their word necessarily carried great weight with the general public. Before long, as a result of united and intelligent effort and of the collecting of evidence that could not be disproved, efforts to have laws, and especially those labor laws covering women workers, revoked by State Legislatures, gradually ceased.

The Government came out with an announcement supporting labor laws and pleading with the states to take no hasty steps to weaken them, except it were at the request of the Council of National Defense. This action had the approval of Mr. Newton Baker, Secretary of War; Mr. Josephus Daniels, Secretary of the Navy, and Mr. Philander Claxton, Commissioner of the Bureau of Education. But, meanwhile, it was necessary to keep an eye upon certain of the Government Departments which were by no means keeping to the Government's declared policy. A striking instance of this was the Government Bureau of Engraving and Printing. It is stated that Director Ralph had had 1,633 girls working overtime; that overtime had been a frequent practice for the previous three years; that 545 of the girls were working from twelve to thirteen hours a day, during which time they received two ten-minute rest periods and two half-hour lunch periods. All this time there were great numbers of competent girls on the Civil Service waiting list. Private employers in the District of Columbia, on the other hand, were compelled to observe the eight-hour day and allow three-quarters of an hour for lunch.

The women's organizations, with the Washington Committee of the National Women's Trade Union League at their head, jointly with the Women's Local of the Bureau of Engraving and Printing, took action. Failing to get prompt results, they laid the facts before Representative Jeannette Rankin of Montana. Miss Rankin paid a surprise visit to the Bureau, satisfied herself that the situation was fully as bad as had been represented, and, from her seat in the House, asked for an investigation. Within less than two weeks the entire force was placed upon an eight-hour basis. In October of the same year the Director of the Bureau, Mr. Joseph Ralph, tendered his resignation. When the new Director had been in office three months the Bureau was turning out more work than ever and with a much smaller staff. This was not because there had been wholesale dismissals, but merely because when girls had left in the ordinary way it had not been found necessary to fill their places.

Early in 1918 the President appointed the Secretary of Labor, Mr. W. B. Wilson, as War Labor Administrator. In order to obtain the counsel of those immediately concerned, he created an Advisory Council to plan with him, and in consultation with the bureau heads of the Department, the War Labor Administration. This accomplished, the activities of the Advisory Council ended. In its design for the War Labor Administration, the Advisory Council provided for the creation of the War Labor Policies Board, to develop plans and policies. It was composed of representatives of all the war branches of the government which have industrial relations.

As recommended by the Advisory Council, the Secretary of Labor, upon the nomination of the presidents of the A. F. of L. and of the National Industrial Conference Board, appointed a War Labor Conference Board, to devise, for the war period, an acceptable method of labor adjustment. The President, in accepting the Board's report, appointed the same persons as a War Labor Board.

The War Labor Conference Board made the first declaration of principles and policy. This became of necessity the guiding policy of the War Labor Board, which was appointed as a result of the Conference Board. The public announcement of the standards by which the War Labor Board would be guided, specifically reserved to both employers and workers the right to organize. It was laid down also that women should be allowed equal pay for equal work, and should not be allotted tasks disproportionate to their strength; that the basic eight-hour day should be recognized as applying in all cases where existing law requires it; in all other cases hours were to be settled with due regard to governmental necessities and the health, welfare and proper comfort of the workers.

The living wage, which was the credo of the war government, is one that may well be recommended to all governments in power in time of peace:

> The right of all workers, including common laborers, to a living wage is hereby declared.
>
> In fixing wages, minimum rates of pay shall be established, which will insure the subsistence of the worker and his family in health and reasonable comfort.

Among the more important appointments allotted to trade union women were these:

Agnes Nestor, glove worker, member of the Advisory Council to the Secretary of Labor, and member of the Woman's Committee under the Council of Defense; Melinda Scott, hat trimmer, Assistant Director in the United States Employment Service; Mary Anderson, boot and shoe worker, Assistant Director of the Woman in Industry Service of the Department of Labor; Elisabeth Christman,

WORKING WOMEN AND THE WAR 193

glove worker, Chief of the Field Representatives of the Woman's Division of the War Labor Board; Florence Thorne, office employe, Assistant Director of the Working Conditions Service of the Department of Labor.*

On the staff of the War Labor Board were a number of examiners, both men and women, whose duty it was to inquire into complaints, and afterwards apply the awards. Miss Marie L. Obenauer was chief of the women examiners. The women investigators, under Miss Elisabeth Christman (glove worker), gathered the facts wherever women workers were involved.

When Miss Mary E. McDowell returned from a trip to France and England, made on behalf of the War Work Council of the National Young Women's Christian Association, she urged upon Miss Van Kleeck the need of finding out statistically what had happened to women after the war and what was the new outlook for women in industry in the United States. There was much information already in the records of the Bureau, but the survey as a whole had to be on a larger scale than the Bureau could undertake. The yearly appropriation of the Women's Bureau was too small to cover such a piece of work, therefore, again at Miss McDowell's suggestion, the survey was financed by the War Work Council. The report, partly based upon statistics secured by federal departments, was revised and condensed by the Women's Bureau and was published in August, 1920, under the title, "The New Position of Women in American Industry." From this report we can build up a picture of what was happening during all the four years in which the war went on, but especially during 1917 and 1918. It was the women already accustomed to the strain

---

* Agnes Nestor and Melinda Scott were included by President Gompers on the Labor Mission sent by the American Federation of Labor to England and France.

and pressure of factory work who were gradually transferred to jobs connected with the war industries. Not infrequently they were transferred as a part of the working force of a factory which had been making cash registers or typewriters, bath-tubs or bird-cages; in many more instances they were taken away from their own job of assembling or packing and put to the actual making of shells, the operating of lathes or the grinding of lenses. But even when all the experienced women workers in the country were thus employed in positions vacated by the drafted men, there was still found room, particularly after the second draft, for tens of thousands of women, many of them married women, who had had no training in any occupation, who had never before worked for wages, but whom employers were only too glad to engage.

The Director of Munitions reported of one plant making gas masks:

> Of the 12,000 employes in this plant, 8,500 were women. . . . The degree of care required in the manufacture of masks was beyond anything in normal industry, . . . after every operation in the manufacture of the face piece, there came an inspection by specially trained women set apart from the operators.

The textile industry was one in which women had always been engaged, and here the results are not so easy to analyze. "Textiles" no longer meant merely material for clothing and house furnishings; it meant canvas for tents, canteen covers, mail bags, covers for tools. Factories which had been making carpets, lace, hose and lamp wicks, turned over their plants entirely to the manufacture of cotton duck and cotton webbing. The new industry of the manufacture of airplanes required silk for parachutes; silk, linen and cotton for airplane wings. In the manufacture of all these

WORKING WOMEN AND THE WAR

goods there was at first a small decrease of women and a larger decrease of men. The women had been drawn into the new war industries, the men had been drafted. Of the women who were employed, almost all continued to do the same kind of work that they had always done, that is, to perform the same or similar processes even though the texture of the woven product might be very different.

A collection of letters from employers on the whole reflect general satisfaction with the work of women. One man, the secretary and treasurer of a metal manufacturing company in Tennessee, wrote:

> Our employes are practically 100 per cent citizens of the United States. The women have replaced men mainly in our sheet metal manufacturing plant. These are paid by the piece, the tasks are accomplished the same as by men, and they are consequently paid the same compensation. They use the same machinery and are equipped the same. We expect to continue employment of women in these occupations. They are given the same training and supervision. We consider them equal to men in point of success.

The president of an electric and manufacturing company in Pennsylvania gave his opinion.

> The number of girls we employed during the war was limited only by the supply. We employed about 2,000 in our main plant and about 300 of these were working in operations which had never been performed by girls before. All the girls who were employed on unusual operations were put through special training rooms, and this practice is being continued. The operations on which we will use women in the future will be determined by the demands upon us and the supply of labor.

In some cases the results were not so happy. From the manager of a manufacturing company in Oregon where the women were sorting and handling light lumber in the planing-mill department, at approximately 80 per cent of the rate paid men:

> We could not say they were either a success or a failure in the experiment, but simply a necessity arising out of the fact that 136 out of our 750 employes went into the service and someone had to take their places. As soon as the necessity passed, we went back to our old program. We do not think women should be or can be successfully employed in lumber manufacturing, although there is a place for them in box factories and other industries connected with the lumber business, where the work is not as heavy as in our operations.

A very careful analysis of a great many letters would be necessary before making too many inferences. Yet there is on the whole no question but that the women made good. Even in the absence of a careful comparison of results on a greater scale than was possible, the following are some of the allowances that must be made: The bulletin points out that the failures were not always chargeable to the women themselves. "Some were clearly due to ill-advised assignments to women to tasks without adequate instruction; others to tasks inherently unsuited to a woman's physique. Loading lumber and wheeling and shoveling coal are among the occupations performed by women as a war emergency, and they do not figure conspicuously among the occupations in which women were recorded as making a success or among those in which women are being retained after the war.

* * * * *

The critical analysis of the results of substitution will show also frequent failures because of marked and obvious deficiencies in equipment and accommodations for women workers. On the other hand, it is not to be expected that among a great number of women drawn into new occupations or new industries, the incompetent, the indifferent and the incorrigible will not be present. The world's wastrels beget girls as well as boys and both make their intermittent trails through industry in war times as well as in peace time. But all of these failures combined do not offer a substantial check to the general stream of evidence of the successful service rendered by wage-earning women in the nation's stern task of equipping its fighting forces with weapons of warfare. The failures from all causes are too few or too inconspicuous to challenge the direct testimony of the War Department or of the employers holding important war orders and making extensive use of woman labor during the war. They are not enough to overcome the evidence of service presented by the increasing numbers of women engaged in new occupations during the war. Least of all do they bulk large enough to contradict the force of evidence borne by the proportion of firms retaining women after the signing of the armistice in the occupations and industries where woman labor was employed at first only as a war emergency."

One very discouraging element in the situation cannot be overlooked. The woman worker had not only to learn a new occupation under conditions of unusual difficulty; she had not only to accustom herself to face novel responsibilities, and often to overcome the masculine prejudice of employers; she had to do all this without the co-operation of her brother workmen, in most cases, in face of their opposition. On this the bulletin is explicit.

In this connection it should be remembered that the machine crafts and other crafts in which women were employed as skilled workers were highly organized; that while women are not usually debarred officially, are in fact often formally eligible to membership—the real attitude toward the admission of women has been one of indifference generally and the attitude toward the extension of woman labor in skilled crafts has often been one of positive hostility. There were some conspicuous exceptions particularly during the war, but the significant fact is that they were exceptions.

The experience of the women car conductors of Cleveland brought before the War Labor Board, to which the press gave nation-wide publicity, is a case in point.

There is nothing so confusing and nothing more paralyzing than diametrically opposite plans of action dealt out to a similar group. A telling instance of this is what has happened to women street car conductors and ticket agents in different cities. During the war, the greatest pressure was brought to bear upon women to enter every occupation stripped for the time of its men employes. One of these occupations was that of conductor on street cars. On the street cars of Cleveland women were first employed in 1917 when the United States Employment Service was advertising the fact that there was a shortage of 36,000 men for the conduct of essential industries in that section of Ohio alone. The women conductors were trained for the work in a training school established by the company because the men conductors refused to teach them. They were paid the same wages and came under all the rules applicable to men. They were self-supporting women, two-thirds of them also supporting children or parents. Twenty-six had husbands or sons in the army. The women conductors' work was primarily that of cashier. The doors of the Cleveland cars open and close with an automatic device upon pressure of a button or else by a light lever which requires but the turning of a hand. The car barns are clean and comfortable, with separate waiting rooms for men and women, the women's department being fitted up neatly as a sitting room and rest room, with a matron in charge. A representative of the National Women's Trade Union League who made inquiry on the ground remarked that there are a dozen kinds of work historically accepted as a "woman's job" which are harder physically, more disagreeable and associated with more undesirable surroundings than was the work of the women conductors of Cleveland.

In spite of these facts, the men of Division 268 of the Amalgamated Association of Street and Railway Employes (Cleveland) demanded the dismissal of the 150 women conductors of the Cleveland Street Railway Company and they actually went out on strike to enforce their demands. The women could not be called scabs, for they had applied for membership in the association. The Amalgamated, however, both through the local and national officers refused to admit the women as members, because to do so would extend to the women protection against dismissal.

The National War Labor Board on December 3, 1918, rendered a decision ordering the dismissal of the women. That it was a dog in the manger policy that the union men were pursuing is evident from the fact that at that very time the Cleveland Street Railway was not running all its cars because it could not obtain the crews to man them.

In Detroit the attitude of the men car conductors was much the same. In Kansas City the union men did not ask for the dismissal of the women, but that they should be guaranteed the same minimum rates as men. This request the War Labor Board supported, and the guarantee was accordingly raised. Later, during a strike called to oblige the Company to accept other conditions in the award, almost all of the women went out with the men. This is an instance of the possibility of co-operation between men and women in the same occupation.

Every age, every country, every social group has had its

own theories as to the work for which women were or are best fitted. The industrial revolution drove women out of the home to follow their traditional occupations, the producing of clothing and the preparation of food. Specialization in many of the machine industries drove other women into machine plants, because they were cheap and readily trained in unskilled processes to replace the former skilled man operative. The enormous development in our own day of transportation and communication created the modern office employments, and women form the great bulk of office employes. Women went into teaching in great numbers for the first time after the Civil War.

It would seem therefore to be self-evident that any very rigid theory as to what is or is not women's vocation in the working world is of very doubtful value, seeing that so many former theories have for this generation passed into forgetfulness. If there is anything unchanging it is the fact of change. Appreciating this it is important to observe that the great and unique change which we can see has already been wrought during the last few years and is already registering its effects on the entire status of the woman worker, has been the opening of a new door, a door that is not likely ever to be closed to many skilled operations for women. This has been of universal evidence. It took place in all of the European countries and was recorded and commented upon in Great Britain even during the first year of the war. This change is one that does not so much show itself in the moving of women from one occupation to another as within the factory or plant itself, where it results in taking the woman away from the mechanical monotonous task of lifting the material used or drilling or feeding the machine to the actual handling of a delicate and complicated machine itself; the milling of the parts, the setting of the machine, the testing of the temper of tools. This is not a difference of trade, it would be noted in no census of industry, it is a change and an elevation in the quality of the work itself; it is a challenge to the woman to show herself worthy of responsibility; an admission that she has latent within her powers and capacities that have never before been called into action.

Whatever promotes a woman to the higher branches of industry makes room for those below her to step up also from their rung in the industrial ladder. The investigators for the Bureau are certain that some at least of the occupations and some of the positions opened to women by war opportunities will continue to be filled by women. At time of writing, the industrial situation is so confused and imperfectly mastered, that it is quite impossible to say just what is happening in the meantime. But an indirect result was seen in the great difficulty the traditional women's trades, the textile and garment trades, had in getting back the women workers after the armistice was declared. The *Textile World Journal* admitted that women had been able to do such good work in new occupations that they were likely to remain on the job even after normal conditions as to labor supply had been restored. The writer considered that only by good wages, sanitation and welfare equipment, could the probable loss of female labor by the textile industries be overcome.

CHAPTER XI

THE NEGRO WOMAN

Negro women were not unaffected by the stepping-up process that during the war had such results upon the occupational status of the white woman. They, oftentimes, sharing in a family migration, left the Southern states to seek for the jobs they heard were so plentiful in the North. Was their home already in the northern industrial cities, then they left domestic and personal services to seek work better paid and under fewer restrictions. As to the white woman, so to her colored sister, the war meant opportunity; it meant an opened door into the world of industrial service. At the same time, radical adjustments were necessary. The colored workers arrived at a northern center, quite unaccustomed to the climate, unprepared as to clothing, as to knowledge of the difficult housing conditions, and untrained in industrial processes.

Among the great mass of reports issued from the official presses there are some few which rank high as human documents. Such an one is "Negro Women in Industry." Not only is it full of information on a subject on which we are most of us quite ignorant, and as indifferent as we are ignorant, but it is in itself a landmark in the slow progress upward of the Negro race.*

---

* Negro Women in Industry Women's Bureau. Department of Labor. 1920. Refer also to the Negro at Work During the World War and Reconstruction. Sec. 19. Division of Negro Economics, United States Department of Labor.

The investigation of the conditions under which the colored woman worked was made and the report written by Miss Emma L. Shields a member of the staff of the Women's Bureau in the Department of Labor with the co-operation of the Bureau of Labor Statistics and of the Division of Negro Economics. Miss Shields was in the field from September to December, 1920. During that time she visited 150 plants, distributed over the states of New York, Pennsylvania, Ohio, Illinois, Michigan, Indiana, Virginia, West Virginia and North Carolina. In these plants were 28,520 women and of these 11,812 were Negro women, or more than forty per cent of all the women employed.

Over half of the Negro women were engaged in the tobacco industry in the rough processes of which they have been taking part for many years. The general effect of the war upon the occupation of Negro women has been noted elsewhere, but this investigation takes us a step further and shows us the colored woman in many occupations hitherto closed to her, and, in some instances at least, still holding her own. To express this moderately, during the brief period that this country was at war, she gained both an industrial experience and a knowledge of the routine working habits of factory life, that have had a distinct effect upon her whole outlook. She has acquired a certain confidence in herself and a "footing, however slippery, which will make her an increasingly important factor in American industry in the future." But more significant still, thirteen of the establishments visited, out of the 150, had employed Negro women for the first time after the war was over. These employers were evidently not driven to engage them through urgent shortage of labor.

The experiences of the women when first entering the clothing industry, were largely those of the newly arrived immigrant on New York's East Side. Many had some idea of sewing but little of what is called the factory sense; the need for punctuality, for keeping their work going so as to fit it in with other processes, and generally adapting themselves to the rigid methods and exacting drills of a manufacturing plant. With many of the workers their first awkwardness gradually passed away and about one-fifth of them were found to be working on the more skilled processes, such as machine operating. In one department of work, and evidence from many other quarters proves this, the Negro women continually surpassed their white sisters, and that was as pressers. No explanation of this has been given. Possibly it was because of actually greater muscular strength or perhaps because colored women have been for so long commonly employed in hand laundry work, with all the hand ironing that it involves.

In the metal industries, almost a new industry to all, these workers, colored and white, came in on the same footing. Most of the women were employed in making cores, sometimes light weight, sometimes heavy cores for stove and automobile castings. The list of operations in all of which women were observed to be occupied, included "drilling, polishing, painting, punch-press operating, moulding, welding, soldering, and filing parts of automobiles, stoves, hardware and enamel products."

The textile industry showed conditions typical of the colored woman's situation. Five establishments employing both white and Negro women, allotted the Negroes such work as scrubbing floors and cleaning lint and cotton from machines. They had no hope of promotion to anything else, as the skilled operations were performed by white women. Four establishments employed only Negro women but they were working on all processes, including the work listed elsewhere as skilled work.

The last of the ten cotton mills visited made no distinction but employed women of both races upon all the operations.

Three managers were anxious to open up better opportunities for the colored women. One of them told of his own discouraging experience in making the attempt. He had employed Negro girls to manufacture cigars in a southern town on an occasion when he found himself in a difficulty for help. His central office objected. The Tobacco Manufacturers' Union brought pressure to bear and he was compelled to abandon the innovation and dispense with his colored assistants, although in his own words, "they made the prettiest, most perfect cigars you ever saw." Similar discrimination existed in every kind of industry that was looked into. Opportunity of employment in the more desirable processes, the pleasanter, cleaner, better paid, more highly skilled, was in the great majority of instances, the privilege of the white women. Was it in the stockyards? The Negro women had to work usually on wet slippery floors where the air was unpleasantly odorous and where there were marked variations in temperature and humidity. In the peanut industry? There was the dragging of weighty and cumbersome bags, heavy and straining work, when it would have been quite possible, with very simple equipment, to lighten the task.

In department stores the colored girl may be a stock girl, an elevator operator or a waitress. So also may the white girl. But a white girl in any of these positions may apply for a job as salesgirl. Of such promotion the colored girl has no hope.

The question of wages is a complicated matter under any circumstances, and the just principle of giving equal pay for equal work, regardless of sex or color, should be insisted on and never lost sight of. The discrimination in wages from which the white woman so generally suffers, applies in an even greater degree to her colored sister. It was often found that there was a great diversity in the pay given to women in different establishments. This inequality was even more marked when the Negro and the white women workers doing identically the same work were separated and working in different buildings. Out of the 150 firms only 32 were employing Negro and white women without separation, with equal opportunities in the work itself and at the same rate of pay. As one Negro woman who had not the good fortune to be employed by one of these firms, said, "You never know what you are going to get; you just take what they give you and go."

The colored woman is so commonly employed in the seasonal trades that the possibility of the stoppage of earnings when the slack season comes on, is with her always a pressing problem, as she is likely to be "the last hired and the first laid off." "You need money to live on in the summer just like you do in the winter," was the unanswerable argument presented.

Several instances of marked efficiency are given that ought to make us pause before accepting the popular view of the inferior capacity of the colored race.

In one large steel plant where the white and Negro girls had started a friendly competition in making cores and filing castings, it was a Negro girl who was considered by the manager as the best worker in the plant. There was her pay envelope for the preceding week, with $38 in it, and it had been known to contain $42.

The superintendent in a large meat packing plant employed Negro women to take the place of men in cutting hog ears, the women to be paid men's wages if they were able to earn them. Of the result he says: "They are paid men's wages and they do the work much better than men did. They seem to be inspired because no difference was made in their wages and their efficiency and regularity on the job has been 100 per cent."

Besides the main question of hours, wages and opportunity, there is the large question of the general adjustment of the colored woman to the new demands that industry for the first time made upon her during the war and to the new opportunities which it also gave to her. These related questions cover employment policies, methods of supervision, education and training of workers. In hiring, transferring and discharging employes there was often no policy at all, or the policy was to leave it entirely to the foreman. He himself would be at a loss because he had had no experience in training such raw workers or in making the adjustments necessary to meet an unfamiliar situation. A grave labor turnover, with all the accompanying waste of time and material, would be the usual result.

Methods of getting around the race difficulty used by different employers were found to be diametrically opposite. In order to conciliate white workers and meet their possible objections to associating with the colored women, some managements placed the latter in separate buildings or workrooms, in some instances even when all were doing the same work. Some of the reasons given were: "Lack of space, and mixed groups wouldn't get along," and "white girls resent proximity to colored girls."

On the other hand there were managers who might almost be living in another country and another age: "I have no separation because it is the policy of the management to promote better racial understanding, and that can only come through contact"; and "I have no separation because where colored and white girls are mixed there is not so much time wasted in visiting. The white girls socialized all the time until I mixed the groups, and now they work and get along beautifully." A practical objection to a separation system is that having to provide separate accommodations and practically a separate plant for two groups burdens the business with needless expense.

A very important point, and one upon which all evidence is agreed, is the desirability of employing Negro forewomen and supervisors wherever there are units of Negro women workers. Closely connected with satisfactory and harmonious supervision is the need of training within the factory. The best one to do the training is a colored woman supervisor, patient, intelligent and willing to hearten and encourage the untrained. Some houses are recognizing this, introducing welfare workers and inviting representatives of community agencies to give educational talks on industrial standards, training courses in home nursing and first aid and adding recreational activities.

Something of the patience and hopefulness of their race was observed in many of the women, and trust and belief in the coming of a new day was frequent. Even in very unpleasant surroundings they could be heard singing and chanting their own songs. A foreman, new to his work, who tried to stop what was to him a most unconventional outlet of energy, was told by his more experienced employer that the women worked better when they sang. From other observers at work in the field of industry for the last few years, come similar stories.

Chicago, the second city industrially, as well as in population, and which has now the third largest Negro population in the country, has been the one that has offered the colored working woman the least opportunity to advance. Though colored girls may learn shorthand, typing and book-keeping in the public schools, most of them are driven to take employment as domestics or janitresses.

While no extensive or thorough survey has been made of Detroit it is certain that a great advance was made in that city in the enlargement of opportunity for colored women workers. The Banner Garment Company has for over five years been running a factory entirely staffed with colored women, from machine operators to clerical employes. During the war they were used to work drill presses in a steel mill. In the automobile plants they were found as assemblers and inspectors, as plate makers in dental laboratories, as armature winders in insulated wire factories, in most of these occupations at the same rate of pay as the white girl. In Detroit also the observation was made that under forewomen of their own race, colored women achieved better results and a higher rate of production.

There are instances on record, as in cartridge factories in Newark, New Jersey, and a bag factory in Decatur, Illinois, where the colored women turned out more cartridges and sewed more bags for the Government than did the white girls. While no one would suggest tests of comparison would have resulted thus, such instances as these go a long way in refuting the familiar charges of general inefficiency set down against the Negro girl.

As regards her permanent industrial status, the colored woman can rise only in the degree her race rises. Unless justice be done to the colored man and woman alike, they will both help to drag down the standards of the white workers to the level of their own, and may live to be registered as strike breakers in many a future struggle.

The general situation has never been more tersely put than by Mary E. McDowell in the *World Tomorrow* for March, 1922.

What shall be the program for those who believe in democracy in industry as well as in politics, and wish a peaceable adjustment in this struggle for a higher standard of living? First, the leader of whites, as well as of blacks, must understand the industrial struggle and the place the colored workers hold in it. The resolutions passed by the Pan African Congress in Belgium last summer recognized this fact.

The American Federation of Labor in 1919 formally decided to open the doors of organized labor unconditionally to Negroes. In 1921 the Chicago Federation of Labor voted, not only to assist but to give a moral and financial aid to the organizing of the colored hotel and restaurant employes. The United Mine Workers of America take colored men into the union without discrimination. In one West Virginia organization, where there are seventy white men and ten Negroes, the president is of the colored group. In Alabama I myself witnessed the loyal stand of the colored miners with the white in a tent colony of brave men and women protesting against bad conditions, while the press called the organizer of the United Mine Workers all the Civil War epithets it could remember. During the late war the local Foundrymen's Union took in their fellow colored workers.

There are many indications that the rank and file are seeing clearly that there must be no discrimination between black and white workers, for those discriminated against will always be the exploited group, and their struggle with the "Iron Man" is a common cause that needs support.

The colored wage earner must be awakened to see that individually he is helpless to change his industrial conditions; he must be made to see himself as a part of the whole struggle; he must be organized and cease being cheap or exploited labor. Organized labor must be made to see its short-sightedness in dealing with colored competitors. If the International Unions do not do their duty, then let the colored people organize themselves and bring pressure on the American Federation of Labor, as I understand is being done by the colored cooks and porters on railroads. The labor struggle must be lifted to a higher plane, for it is too much physical and too little spiritual. An intelligent public opinion must be created through the education of the teachers and social workers, the colleges and the ministry. The leaders must be led to see the significance to the colored group of workers, both men and women, of the struggle of labor for a higher standard of living.

Inter-racial committees in the South and North have a special duty to perform to protect society from this inter-racial clashing in industry. Leaders must know the "Iron Man" and protect the weak from his power.

"Public opinion is the greatest of all the powers"; therefore, create public opinion and organize the colored workers.

Chapter XII

INTERNATIONAL FEDERATION OF WORKING WOMEN

The National Women's Trade Union League of America took the initial steps toward an international meeting of working women at its convention in Kansas City in 1917, when the delegates appealed to the organized working women of all countries to co-operate in calling an international congress of working women to be held at the same time as the first International Labor Conference. At the same gathering the question of uniform international labor standards came up.

The only basis upon which international commercial competition can be conducted fairly and without injustice to the workers is by the setting up of common standards of hours and payment. The White Goods Workers of Paris (Syndicat General de la Chemiserie, Lingerie, etc.) presented through Madame Gabrielle Duchene a plan which the convention unanimously endorsed, asking for the insertion into the treaty of peace to be signed at the close of the war, of labor clauses, to apply to every country which is a party to the treaty, and to take effect within a definite time. These labor clauses to prescribe "standards covering conditions of work, the hours of work and the wages paid, so that the workers may be insured such elementary rights as the eight-hour day, one day rest in seven, no child labor, the abolition of night work for women, a living wage in proportion to the cost of living in each country, and equal pay for equal work."

Yet further developments of the same idea were:—the insistence by the signatory governments of equally high standards in all government contracts; the creation of labor bureaus in every country and of one international bureau, to be a clearing house for all information on labor questions, and maintaining the standards which the various countries should have bound themselves to observe.

As soon as the Armistice was signed the League's Committee on Social and Industrial Reconstruction met in New York and urged the early calling together of an International Congress of Working Women for the exchange of thought and the concerted action required by the task before all women, and drew up proposed international standards.

In order to come into close touch with the European situation, and to put the working women's view before the International Labor Conference of the League of Nations, the National Women's Trade Union League, early in 1919, sent Miss Mary Anderson and Miss Rose Schneiderman to Paris. While passing through London, they conferred with Miss Margaret Bondfield, Assistant Secretary of the Federation of Women Workers. In Paris, it was their intention to present to the Labor Commission, organizing the conference, the standards drawn up by the League's Committee on Social and Industrial Reconstruction, and also two amendments prepared by the British labor women, urging women advisers in the Labor Conference, and also that there should be women officials in the International Labor Office. Unfortunately, owing to the many delays in the journey, and complications as to the viséing of passports by at least three separate consulates, the two delegates did not reach their destination until the day after the Labor Commission had disbanded, and any action they could take was then purely informal. Their visit, however, was the means of accomplishing a great deal. Their very presence did much to rouse keen interest in a possible working women's international meeting, not as something in the far future, but within the next few months, and with all the prestige of being held in connection with the first meeting of the International Labor Conference. The labor officials moreover could not fail to realize that after all, there was a woman's point of view.

At the following convention of the National Women's Trade Union League in Philadelphia in June, 1919, plans were completed and delegates elected. Shortly after steps were taken to invite the delegates from other nations to meet with the league's delegates in Washington, and to meet ahead of the official Labor Conference of the League of Nations, in order to place before that body the well considered recommendations of the working women of the world. All delegates were asked to produce credentials signed by the trade union organizations of their respective countries. They were also asked to prepare material on child labor, on women's employment, the eight-hour day, unemployment and the care of maternity. Delegates attended representing twelve nations, Argentina, Belgium, the British Empire, Canada, Czecho-Slovakia, France, India, Italy, Norway, Poland, Sweden and the United States.

Several of the foreign delegates also held the position of technical adviser to the delegations of their respective countries in the International Labor Conference at Washington. There were besides other women technical advisers, who although not delegates to the Working Women's Congress attended many of its sessions and took part in the discussions. Still others came as visitors. Among this unofficial group were women from Cuba, Denmark, Italy, Japan, the Netherlands, Poland, Serbia, Spain, Sweden and Switzerland.

The two youngest republics represented, Czecho-Slovakia and Poland, sent delegates who were representatives of their country not only as workers, but in its public life. There was Madame Stychova, a member of the National Assembly of Czecho-Slovakia, and Madame Majerova of the City Council of Prague, while Mlle. Konopska, one of the Polish delegates, an embroidery worker, had been candidate for the Polish Parliament on a labor ticket at a recent election.

During the week of October 28 to November 6, 1919, the delegates discussed industrial standards considered internationally. They drew up a set of international resolutions, expressing their demands upon those subjects, and presented these demands to the men of thirty-four nations who were holding the official International Labor Conference of the League of Nations just a few blocks away.

There were no women delegates attending that conference, which supplied an additional reason why an International Congress of Working Women had to be held. It is satisfactory to know that the women's resolutions won at least a respectful hearing at the official conference.

"At a very early stage of the proceedings the Congress took the opportunity of passing on to the Labor Conference the desire of women everywhere that they should have direct representation at the next Labor Conference; and that every country should be represented by at least one woman delegate. To be a technical adviser is all very well, but the power of the woman technical adviser is entirely dependent upon the good will of the man delegate whom she is appointed to assist. If he chooses she may have the floor, and exercise his vote upon any question involving women, and if he does not so choose, she must sit in unworthy suppression and silence, while the industrial rights of her sister women may be voted away."

The subjects covered the eight-hour day with the fifty-four-hour week (for all workers), child labor, maternity insurance, night work, unemployment, hazardous occupations, immigration and the distribution of raw materials. The Congress also provided for its own continuous existence through a provisional committee consisting of the President, vice-presidents and secretary and treasurer, with correspondents in the various nations and with an international office in the United States.

The lines along which differences between the delegates presented themselves could have been foreseen by no one. To the suggestion of maternity insurance in principle, every delegate was ready with an eager assent. But it presently developed that the vote would turn largely upon details. In every case, when the point was driven home, it was shown that the decision of each delegate upon the form it should take, depended very largely on the needs of her own country. On the point of having the very best medical and surgical and nursing care during childbirth, and having it free, there was encouraging unanimity; but the women from the poorer countries hesitated long before they would agree to a cash benefit as well. "Our countries are so poor; how can they pay it?" was the pitiful plaint. The larger view that prevailed among women coming from the less oppressed lands was that such benefit and such care should be for all mothers, this being the only way in which the stigma of charity could be removed, the ability on the part of a few to pay for it being regarded as merely an irrevelant and altogether insignificant feature. Again came the protest "Our country cannot pay for a single woman who has the means to provide for herself." It was then proposed to make the matter part of a general health insurance scheme. But no, "Unless my country does it through the state as a separate affair, it will not be done at all." So that too was left to the individual nations to determine.

It was an astonishing program that was presented by the Polish delegates, not at all what would have been expected from such simple women. It was nothing less than a world table, a world market, world industry. They asked for equal distribution of the "raw materials existing in the world, as well as the international control of maritime transports which determine the increase of price of the raw material." Truly an end to blockades; an end to hogging of sugar, to profiteering in meat or in cotton, an end to hoarding for a better price; the little poor country to have a fair chance along with the great and rich commercial empires. The same with labor and labor's opportunities. Few of the poor cross the seas for adventure; they make the journey to get work, and so are made the means of the exploitation of others, who have to make room in the labor market for those poorer and less well-equipped than themselves, save in the dangerous ability to live on little. Away with all this, said the Poles. Let immigration and unemployment be regulated internationally, labor departments and trade unions having a say in how both workers and work had best be allotted to the various regions and countries.

At this Congress, the first world gathering of working women ever held, the idea was in the air that it was not only an international gathering, but it was also a meeting of internationalists. Strange to say it was hardly that. Such can scarcely be said yet of any gathering, drawn from any group, labor, socialist, or any other. Our present experiences are only an illustration of the well-proved axiom "We learn by doing." Very few, either delegates or onlookers, had yet reached the international viewpoint, though all sincerely intended to think and to speak and to vote as world citizens. The nearest approach to this was a conscientious and unflinching determination to be fair and tolerant. It is to the credit of all that fairness and tolerance were habitually shown through the most trying and testing discussions. But the fact remains that this constant repression in themselves, by delegates, of their own naturally aggressive patriotism is a negative virtue only and still a long way from the internationalism at which they are aiming.

As the only way to learn is by doing, so the only way to become internationalists is to internationalize, to meet, to confer, and to meet again, to thrash out difficulties, to become acquainted with each other's national peculiarities and national needs.

The international viewpoint is nevertheless essential in these tentative beginnings toward mutual understanding. Internationalism is the result of meeting and conferring, and the consciousness of international unity is by no means necessary to its gradual growth. Internationalism itself is the outgrowth of the conflict of ideas, of meeting and making a workable compromise. The creation of the thing itself in this slow fashion is a greater achievement than any of the definite results or than any of the compromises by which it is attained.

This has evidently been the experience of others besides working women. Every group which has met during the last five years seems to have appreciated this, in one degree or another, and the fact was openly accepted by many of the delegates to the conference on the Limitation of Armaments.

As the Polish delegates spoke that fall day, the listener might feel in fancy a fresher air, a clearer atmosphere. Yet it was their own awful necessity, the crying need for raw materials, the knowledge that some of them might have to fare forth to seek work in richer countries, that had sharpened their wits in thinking out these plans to restore the home and family life in Poland. The plan, conceived on a scale of international significance originated in the hopeless situation of a starving and exhausted country that must have the raw materials of existence and of industry, or perish. But even so they were far ahead of the old nationalism. A few years ago, in similar straits, the Poles would have asked for some favored nation clause or through some other scheme, have tried to secure an opening into the field of commercial and industrial prosperity. Now, given the opportunity to think internationally they laid out their plan on international lines, and they proposed to plan for the whole world on the lines that they knew to be for their own country's good.*

The next two years were busy ones for the Bureau of the International Working Women's Congress—its headquarters were in Washington. Mrs. Raymond Robins as president, Mrs. Maud Swartz as secretary, and Miss Miriam Shepherd as executive secretary, gradually built up connections with the working women's groups in all the civilized countries, and in some just on the borderland of that uncertain standard that we call civilization. The various correspondents pooled their ideas in the central office, and out of it all grew gradually a draft constitution and plans for effective co-operation with the next International Labor Conference to be held in Geneva. So that it was with a well prepared program before them that the delegates assembled in Geneva on October 17, 1921.

* A report of the First International Congress of Working Women, by Miss Vera Schaefer and the writer, in *Life and Labor* for December, 1919, has been freely drawn upon.

The Washington Conference had been a preliminary gathering, an open meeting. The Geneva Congress was from beginning to end a series of business sessions in which very genuine results were achieved; much of this was accomplished during the long hours spent by the commissions (or committees) in working out a basis for the organization and in formulating resolutions which were practical and ignored none of the difficulties ahead. Geneva was more real than Washington and in every way further ahead because the women were actually taking hold, preparing to stand by one another and to carry out the plans decided upon. They were facing steadily their many obligations, to their own country, to the trade union movement and to the women of the world. It was a difficult hour in Europe, and it was remarkable that a group with such a varied background could unite on a program. Yet there was closer understanding and co-operation between the women of different nationalities. The Congress itself, instead of being on a provisional footing was placed on a solid basis. The name of the Congress was changed from International Congress to International Federation of Working Women and a plan was arranged for a system of dues to meet the expenses of running the Bureau and holding the next conference. Although only twelve nations are in actual affiliation, thirty nations were represented in Geneva. The delegates were:

*Belgium......Helene Burniaux, Syndical du Parti Ouvrier et teacher. des Syndicats Independents

---

* These four delegates from the Christian Unions of Belgium found it impossible to accept the Constitution adopted by the International Congress of Working Women because of the affiliation with the International Federation of Trade Unions at Amsterdam, and they withdrew from the Congress. They have their own federation of Christian Unions.

FEDERATION OF WORKING WOMEN 221

	Victorie Cappe.......	Commission Inter-Syndical Feminine Chretienne de Belgique.
	Julie de Lauw........	Commission Inter-Syndical Feminine Chretienne de Belgique.
	Berthe de Lalieux....	Commission Inter-Syndical Feminine Chretienne de Belgique.
Cuba..........	Laura de Zayas Bazan	Syndicato de Fogoneros, Marinos y Similares.
Czecho-Slovakia.	Bozena Kubickova....	Ceskoslovenske Obec Delnicke.
	J. Linhartova........	Sekretariat zen Ceskoslav Socialne Demokratioke Strany Delnicke.
France........	Eugenie Berruelle, garment worker.	Fédération des Travailleurs de l'Habillement de France, et des Colonies.
	Georgette Bouillot, embroiderer.	Confédération Generale du Travail.
	Jeanne Bouvier......	Confédération Generale du Travail.
	Jeanne Chevenard, textile worker.	Confédération Generale du Travail.
	Henriette Coulmy garment worker.	Fédération des Travailleurs de l'Habillement de France, et des Colonies.
	Suzanna Gibault, office worker.	Fédération Nationale des Syndicats d'Employés.
Great Britain...	Mrs. Harrison Bell....	Standing Joint Committee of Women's Industrial Organizations.
	Margaret Bondfield...	Standing Joint Committee of Women's Industrial Organizations.
	Edith H. House, telephone operator.	Standing Joint Committee of Women's Industrial Organizations.
	Thirza Livesley, textile worker.	Standing Joint Committee of Women's Industrial Organizations.

	Kate Manicom, Workers' union.	Standing Joint Committee of Women's Industrial Organizations.
	Edith McDonald, clerk.	Standing Joint Committee of Women's Industrial Organizations.
	Marion Phillips......	Standing Joint Committee of Women's Industrial Organizations.
	Mrs. Bell Richards...	Standing Joint Committee of Women's Industrial Organizations.
	Madeleine Symons....	Standing Joint Committee of Women's Industrial Organizations.
Italy..........	Laura Casartelli Cabrini.	Federazione Italiana fra Operai Tessili and other organizations.
Norway.......	Ingeborg Drolsum....	Kristiana Kvindelige Handelsbunds Forening.
	Laura Delphin Holm, Office Workers' Union.	Kristiana Kvindelige Handelsbunds Forening.
	Louise Kleve, agricultural worker.	Barums Smaahrukerlag, Kristiana.
	Betzy Kjelsberg......	Kvindelige Telegraffunktionarers Landsforbudd, Kristiana.
Poland........	Sophie Dobrzanska...	Comite Central Polonais pour les Affaires du Congres.
South Africa...	Mrs. Mary Fitzgerald.	South African Industrial Federation.
Switzerland....	Angele Monnier, watchmaker.	L'Union Syndicale Suisse.
United States...	Sarah Green.........	National Women's Trade Union League of America.
	Mrs. Raymond Robins.	National Women's Trade Union League of America.
	Emma Steghagen.....	National Women's Trade Union League of America.
	Maud Swartz........	National Women's Trade Union League of America.

FEDERATION OF WORKING WOMEN

Among visitors, Mrs. Weaver and Miss Sophie Sanger represented the International Labor Office; Fraulein Gertrud Baer, the Women's International League for Peace and Freedom; Miss Mary Dingman, the World's Young Women's Christian Association; Mme. Chaponniere-Chaix, the International Council of Women; Mme. Antoinette Girardet-Veille, the International Woman Suffrage Alliance. From Roumania came Mme. Ramneceanu, Union Mondiale de la Femme; from China, Miss We Tsung Zung, a Y. W. C. A. worker, and from Japan, Mrs. Moto Matsumato and Miss Toshi Nagasawa of the Nippon Women's University of Tokio.

In discussing the new constitution, it was not hard to agree upon the object to "unite organized women in order that they may resolve upon the means by which the standard of the life of the workers throughout the world may best be raised." There was also unanimity as to the three principal methods of carrying out that object.

a. To promote trade union organization among women.
b. To develop an international policy giving special consideration to the needs of women and children, and examine closely all projects for legislation proposed by the League of Nations, and especially by the International Labor Conferences.
c. To promote the appointment of women to represent organized working women on all organizations and committees dealing with questions affecting the welfare of the workers.

A program surely eminently practical, sane and conservative.

Profound differences of opinion, however, presently developed upon the basis of membership, and the definition of membership finally decided upon must be considered quite a triumph of tolerance as well as diplomacy, meeting, as it does, almost contrary situations in different countries and fitting itself so as to harmonize with the internal policies of the labor movement in the several countries.

> The Federation shall consist of National Trade Union organizations, containing women members, and affiliated to the International Federation of Trade Unions; it shall also admit working women's organizations accepting its aims and agreeing to work in the spirit and to follow the principles of the International Federation of Trade Unions.

This phrasing satisfied the British delegates, who felt that they could join no organization which would exclude any branch of their tri-party labor movement with its trade union, its political, and its co-operative wings. It could be accepted by the most conservative French delegates, because it admitted the leadership in western Europe today of the (Amsterdam) International Federation of Trade Unions, and can be presented for acceptance to the German labor women, as they, too, accept the leadership of Amsterdam. The American delegation was the most flexible among the representatives of the larger countries and to it this definition of membership proved entirely satisfactory. Any controversy which may arise between conferences as to eligibility will be decided by the Executive Board, who shall submit the decision to the next congress.

The number of delegates allowed to each nation is one thing; its voting strength another. Each national organization is entitled to send five delegates for the first fifty thousand women or less, and one additional delegate for each additional fifty thousand or part thereof. In voting, on the other hand, there is to be one vote for each national organization of fifty thousand or less. All organizations above fifty thousand are allowed two votes, and no more than two, whatever their numbers.

FEDERATION OF WORKING WOMEN 225

The main program of the congress was the agenda of the International Labor Conference, sitting in Geneva, including prevention of anthrax, raising standards of agricultural workers and the international causes of unemployment.

How essential are such international labor conferences was strikingly illustrated in the discussion on the prevention of anthrax. To most Americans the disease means little, and yet the disease so entitled is one whose spread cannot be checked, save through international action. It is primarily a disease of certain animals, in particular of the sheep. Human beings become infected through the handling of infected wool, hides, hair or fur. If infected wool or other animal product be not disinfected before leaving the port of origin, the deadly spores remain dormant to threaten the lives of any worker, say, in the textile industry, through whose hands the material may pass in course of manufacture. The disease can be communicated through the most unimportant cut or abrasion on the unfortunate worker's hands and manifests itself in the form of boils, ending in blood poisoning, often fatal. Miss Thirza Livesley, a textile worker from Bradford, England, appealed to the delegates to pass the resolution providing for measures of control and thus help to stamp out this pestilence.

Besides requesting efficient disinfection at any port where large quantities of wool are handled, the Commission asked for scientific investigation which would aim at preventing entirely the occurrence of this disease in the animal victim and mentioned that in one nation or another steps have already been taken to deal with "dangerous wool." The British Government has established an experimental station for disinfection at Liverpool and at least one other country has already passed legislation prohibiting the importation of scheduled dangerous wool. The Commission made the significant suggestion that any international committee set up should include in addition to Government representatives a substantial number of trade unionists.

One of the most vital questions discussed was that of shortening the hours and raising the industrial standards and living conditions of agricultural workers. The Congress took issue with the governments of France and Switzerland, which have decided that workers in agricultural pursuits do not come under the control of the International Labor Organization of the League of Nations. It was voted that workers in agriculture should have the same status regarding hours as workers in factories, offices and shops. One American delegate who had not been quite disposed to think too highly of her own country's slow rate of progress was more than shocked to learn what were the standards that have come down to present day Europe from the ages, so that it was necessary to solemnly pass a law saying that agricultural workers must not sleep in barns and stables. The concluding clauses of the resolution asked that agricultural workers should have the same right to combine as industrial workers and that they be protected against accident, illness, disablement and old age, with distinct provision for the care of country women during maternity.

The present crisis in unemployment, the delegates declared, is mainly due to international causes, and therefore can only be solved by the re-establishment of a normal world trade. With this end in view they called upon all countries to take concerted action for the stabilization of the value of money and the exchange rates between different countries, and also the extension of credits. They asked, too, that each country should handle intelligently the problem of unemployment within its own borders; that the state should care for the unemployed; that long hours and overtime should be abolished; that the possibilities of

FEDERATION OF WORKING WOMEN 227

women's work should be carefully considered, both from the side of training and the possibility of permanent employment. Finally, the Congress maintained that the cultivation of new lands and better methods of cultivation would greatly lessen unemployment.

It was a young woman who led the Congress on the question of disarmament. Miss Kate Manicom, of the Workers' Union of Great Britain, spoke on behalf of the young women of the world, many of whom must themselves be denied the possibility of motherhood:

We in this conference feel that we can be the mothers of the world. We realize that these great misunderstandings have been responsible for all of the wars of the world. We will try to prevent with all the force of nature any repetition of the horrors we have just come through.

Miss Manicom was deputed to carry to President Harding and to the Washington Conference on the Limitation of Armaments, then about to convene, a message asking for total disarmament.*

Miss Gertrude Baer, a young German girl, fraternal delegate from the Women's International League for Peace and Freedom, told how the army in Germany had been reduced to one hundred thousand men, an army for defense only.

More and more, as session succeeded session, was evident the great desire of the women to come together. More and more did they begin to recognize their common ignorance of the limitations and opportunities of their different coun-

---

* Miss Manicom fulfilled her mission as one of a committee of nationally representative women who brought to President Harding on November 14, 1921, the pledge of women of over twenty nations in the support of his effort to turn the mind of the world to the abolition of war.

tries. How much had been accomplished two years before in the way of building up mutual confidence and friendship was evident in the close sense of co-operation between those women who had worked together then in Washington.

One of the greatest barriers to ready and perfect understanding between national representatives on these occasions is the barrier of language. As a step toward removing that barrier, the French delegates in particular were insistent that all delegates to a future congress should be able to speak Esperanto, and that either Esperanto or some other form of expression selected as a universal language should be taught in the public schools of every country secondary only to the native tongue.

The headquarters of the International Federation of Working Women was set in London; the secretary, Dr. Marion Phillips, an Australian, long resident in England; Mrs. Harrison Bell, also of England, the treasurer. Mrs. Raymond Robins remains president. The vice-presidents are:

Belgium	Helene Burniaux
Canada	Mrs. Katherine Derry
Cuba	Mrs. Laura de Zayas Bazan
Czecho-Slovakia	Mrs. Bozena Kubickova
France	Jeanne Bouvier
Great Britain	Margaret Bondfield
Italy	Laura Cabrini Casartelli
Norway	Mrs. Betzy Kjelsberg
Poland	Sophie Dobrzanska
South Africa	Mrs. Mary Fitzgerald
Switzerland	Angela Monnier
United States	Mrs. Maud Swartz

At the Third Biennial Congress of the International Federation of Working Women, in Vienna, August, 1923, Mrs. Raymond Robins declining re-election, Mdlle. Helene Burniaux of Belgium was elected president, the secretary being Miss Edith McDonald of London.

Chapter XIII

CONCLUSION

Women trade unionists meet with the same difficulties, attain the same successes, and have to solve the same problems as men, with certain complications in addition. Whatever is encouraging in the labor outlook, they share. Whatever new responsibilities are accepted by the labor movement as a whole, they must share. Whatever developments, anticipated or unlooked for, may come to pass, will affect women as well as men.

In the unorganized or the poorly organized trades, there are great improvements needed in wages, hours and working conditions. To obtain these improvements is the first aim of the labor organizer. On this efforts must be concentrated.

In the trades in which there are a number of local unions, and at least a strong nucleus of organized establishments, the situation is different. The typographical unions, the unions of waitresses and some others report that though their trade may not be one hundred per cent organized (that happy state being still in the distance) they have in other directions accomplished more than they at first set out to do. Emulation between competing establishments in the same center, and rivalry between employers for competent help has in many cities resulted in so raising the standards of all that the union has now actually less to offer than before. It becomes more difficult to attract the girl into the union, or to organize the restaurant, because she may be already receiving the union wage, working the union hours, and at the same time is not called on to pay any dues. While this is from one angle, encouraging, from another the situation is more baffling.

The inference is not the ready and superficial one, that organization has done its work, and is no longer required in such occupations. Were the unions to slack on their job, standards would soon be lowered. It is now, therefore, the part of labor to bring into play new motives, to supply their members with fresh interests, and to study what those members desire, beyond the primary wants of better economic conditions.

What has most to be fought is the force of inertia, as formidable an obstacle to advance in women as in men. Nothing can cope with this as manifested among the workers themselves, except the vitalizing of the whole labor movement, by the stimulus of education, the making use of all the untouched possibilities, the energy, the ability that lie unsuspected in numbers of working men and women. It will largely be experiment. No one yet knows how far individual leaders must shoulder responsibility, or just how actively the rank and file will function, and function effectively.

It is for the members to say what they seek, for the leaders to help them in the search, and to satisfy the needs, expressed or only half conscious. There may be channels of expression which experience only can discover. At present there are at least several known ways in which trade unionism is developing, and through which it is inspiring its membership and calling forth their latent powers: the co-operative movement, the movement for fitting themselves to take part in the control of industry, the educational movement, and the political movement.

If any one of these new developments is to hold the promise of the future, it must grow among the young.

CONCLUSION

Therefore it is to the young, young women and young men that the future of the labor movement is committed. May they find their inspiration in the words of the late John Davidson.

TO THE GENERATION KNOCKING AT THE DOOR

Break—break it open: let the knocker rust;
Consider no "shalt not," and no man's "must";
And, being entered, promptly take the lead,
Setting aside tradition, custom, creed:
Nor watch the balance of the huckster's beam:
Declare your hardiest thought, your proudest dream:
Await no summons: laugh at all rebuff:
High hearts and youth are destiny enough.
The mystery and the power enshrined in you
Are old as time and as the moment new:
And none but you can tell the part you play,
Nor can you tell until you make assay,
For this alone, this always will succeed,
The miracle and magic of the deed.

SOURCE LIST OF REFERENCES AND READING

Abbott, Edith, WOMEN IN INDUSTRY, *Appleton*, 1910.

Abbott, Grace, THE IMMIGRANT AND THE COMMUNITY, *Century Co.*, 1917.

Amalgamated Clothing Workers, New York, PUBLICATIONS OF.

American Federation of Labor History, ENCYCLOPEDIA AND REFERENCE BOOK, 1919.

American Federationist (monthly), Newsletter (weekly), *A. F. of L., Washington, D. C.*

American Labor Year Book, VOLS. I, II, III, IV, 1916-1922, *Rand School of Social Science.*

Andrews, Irene Osgood and Hobbs, Margaretta A., ECONOMIC EFFECTS OF THE WAR UPON WOMEN AND CHILDREN IN GREAT BRITAIN, *Carnegie Endowment for International Peace*, 1918.

Andrews, John B. and Bliss, W. P. D., HISTORY OF WOMEN IN TRADE UNIONS IN THE UNITED STATES, *Vol. X of the United States Report on the Condition of Woman and Child Wage Earners.*

Andrews, John B., LABOR PROBLEMS AND LABOR LEGISLATION, *American Association for Labor Legislation*, 1919.

d'Arusmont, Frances Wright, BIOGRAPHY AND NOTES OF, *Boston*, 1848.

Beard, Mary, A SHORT HISTORY OF THE AMERICAN LABOR MOVEMENT, *Workers' Education Bureau*, 1922 Series.

Brandeis, Louis D., M. B. Hammond, John A. Hobson, Elizabeth C. Watson, Howard B. Woolston, CASE FOR MINIMUM WAGE, A SYMPOSIUM, *The Survey*, Feb. 6, 1915.

Brown, Rome G., THE MINIMUM WAGE (in opposition), *Minneapolis* 1, 1912.

Budish, J. M. and Soule, George, THE NEW UNIONISM, *Harcourt Brace and Howe*, 1920.

Cohen, Rose, OUT OF THE SHADOW, *Doran*, 1918.

Commons, John R., Andrews, John B., Sumner, Helen L. and others, DOCUMENTARY HISTORY OF AMERICAN INDUSTRIAL SOCIETY, *Arthur H. Clark Co., Cleveland*, 1910.

Commons, John R. and Associates, HISTORY OF LABOR IN THE UNITED STATES, *Macmillan*, 1918.

SOURCE LIST

Commons, John R. and Andrews, John B., PRINCIPLES OF LABOR LEGISLATION, REVISED EDITION, *Harper*, 1920.
Delzell, Ruth, EARLY WOMEN TRADE UNIONISTS, *National Women's Trade Union League* (Pamphlet).
Derry, Katherine and Douglas, Paul H., MINIMUM WAGE LAWS IN CANADA, *Journal of Political Economy, April,* 1922.
Fraser, Helen, WOMEN AND WAR WORK, *Shaw,* 1918.
Goldmark, Josephine, FATIGUE AND EFFICIENCY, *Russell Sage Foundation,* 1911.
Heaton, H., THE BASIC WAGE PRINCIPLE IN AUSTRALIAN WAGE REGULATION, *Economic Journal, London, September,* 1921.
Henry, Alice, THE TRADE UNION WOMAN, *Appleton,* 1915.
Hewes, Amy, and Walter, Henriette R., WOMEN AS MUNITION-MAKERS, *Russell Sage Foundation,* 1917.
Hutchinson, Emilie J., WOMEN'S WAGES, *Longman,* 1919.
Kellor, Frances A., OUT OF WORK, *Putnam, Second Edition* (1915).
Lilienthal, Meta Stern, FROM FIRESIDE TO FACTORY (Booklet), *Rand School Book-Shop,* 1916.
Lowie, R. H., PRIMITIVE SOCIETY, *Boni and Liveright,* 1920.
Marot, Helen, AMERICAN LABOR UNIONS, *Holt,* 1914.
Mason, Otis T., WOMAN'S SHARE IN PRIMITIVE CULTURE, *Appleton,* 1894.
Matthews, Lillian R., WOMEN IN TRADE UNIONS IN SAN FRANCISCO, *University of California,* 1913.
National Consumers' League, New York, PUBLICATIONS OF.
National Women's Trade Union League of America, Chicago, Publications of, including:—LIFE AND LABOR, 1911-1921, LIFE AND LABOR BULLETIN (monthly), PROCEEDINGS OF CONVENTIONS, 1909-1911-1913-1915-1917-1919-1922, OTHER LITERATURE.
National Woman's Party, PUBLICATIONS OF, *Washington, D. C.*
Owen, Robert, LIFE OF ROBERT OWEN, NEW EDITION, *Knopf,* 1920.
Owen, Robert Dale, THREADING MY WAY, *Carleton-Trübner,* 1874.
Peixotto, Jessica B., WOMEN OF CALIFORNIA AS TRADE UNIONISTS, *Association of Collegiate Alumnae, December,* 1908.
Perkins, Charlotte Gilman, WOMEN AND ECONOMICS, *Small Maynard,* 1898.
Rathbone, Eleanor, WAGES ACCORDING TO FAMILY NEEDS, *Economic Journal (London), December,* 1920.
Ryan, John A., A LIVING WAGE IN ITS ETHICAL AND ECONOMIC ASPECTS, *Macmillan,* 1906.

Savage, Marion Dutton, INDUSTRIAL UNIONISM IN AMERICA, *Ronald Press*, 1922.

Schreiner, Olive, WOMAN AND LABOUR, *Stokes*, 1911.

Simons, A. M., SOCIAL FORCES IN AMERICAN HISTORY, *Macmillan*, 1914.

Spencer, Anna Garlin, THE FAMILY AND ITS MEMBERS, *Lippincott*, 1923.

Sumner, Helen L., WOMEN IN INDUSTRY, *Volume IX of the United States Report on the Condition of Woman and Child Wage Earners.*

Thomas, W. I., SEX AND SOCIETY, *University of Chicago Press*, 1907.

Tyler, J. M., THE GREAT STONE AGE IN NORTHERN EUROPE, *Scribner*, 1921.

United States Census of 1920, OCCUPATIONAL STATISTICS.

Veblen, Thorstein B., THE INSTINCT OF WORKMANSHIP, *Macmillan*, 1914.

Waggaman, Mary T., NATIONAL WOMEN'S TRADE UNION LEAGUE OF AMERICA, *Monthly Labor Review*, April, 1919.

Wolfe, F. E., ADMISSION TO AMERICAN TRADE UNIONS, CHAPTER IV, *Johns Hopkins Press*, 1912.

Wolman, Leo, EXTENT OF TRADE UNIONISM, *Annals of the Amer. Acad. of Political and Social Science, Vol. 69, January,* 1917.

Wolman, Leo, AN OUTLINE OF THE AMERICAN LABOR MOVEMENT (Pamphlet Series No. 2), *Workers Education Bureau of America.*

Wolman, Leo, and others, THE CLOTHING WORKERS OF CHICAGO. *Joint Board, Chicago,* 1922.

Women's Bureau, Department of Labor, Washington, D. C., Publications of, ANNUAL REPORTS. Bulletins, including among others: WOMEN IN INDUSTRY, HOME WORK IN BRIDGEPORT, CONNECTICUT, HOURS AND CONDITIONS OF WORK FOR WOMEN IN INDUSTRY IN VIRGINIA, WOMEN IN GOVERNMENT SERVICE, INDUSTRIAL OPPORTUNITIES AND TRAINING FOR WOMEN AND GIRLS, THE NEW POSITION OF WOMEN IN AMERICAN INDUSTRY, WAGES FOR WORKING WOMEN IN KANSAS, NEGRO WOMEN IN INDUSTRY, FAMILY STATUS OF BREADWINNING WOMEN, THE OCCUPATIONAL PROGRESS OF WOMEN, THE WOMEN IN THE CANDY INDUSTRY, ALSO CHARTS, POSTERS, MAPS, TABLES OF STATE LEGISLATION, ETC., *Government Printing Office, Washington.*

INDEX

A

Abramovitch, Bessie, 121
Actors, 93
American Federation of Labor, 98
Anderson, Mary, 97, 121, 174, 213
Anthony, Susan B., 53

B

Baer, Gertrude, 227
Baker, Secretary of War, 114
Bagley, Sarah G., 45, 46
Barnum, Gertrude, 75, 110
Barry, Leonora M., 51
Barrymore, Ethel, 94
Basic Wage Commission in Australia, 157
Bensley, Martha (Mrs. Robert Bruere), 75
Bibliography, 232
Black list, 46
Board of Education, Chicago, 80
Bondfield, Margaret, 213
Borland, Representative, of Missouri, 91
Brandeis, Louis D., 130, 147, 148
Bryn Mawr Summer School, 115
Brophy, Dora, 75
Bureau of Labor Statistics, 203
Burke, Mary, 53

C

Cahill, Helen, 98
Carey, Mathew, 41
Carleton, Mary H., 46
Child labor, 214, 216
Children's Bureau, 168, 169
Christman, Elisabeth, 98
Cohn, Fannia, 82, 97

Colonial Woman, the, 31–36
  business activities, 35–36
  child labor, 35
  domestic production, 32
  economic position, 34
  her occupation, 33
  home industries, 32
  spinning schools, 35
Conboy, Sara A., 7
Congress, 91
Conference on the Limitation of Armaments, 227
Constitution, 224
Czecho-Slovakia, 215

D

Daley, Margaret, 97
Deaths in childbirth, 169
Dempsey, Mary, 98
Department of Commerce and Labor, 166
Department of Labor, 166
Division of Negro Economics, 203
Dodge, Grace, 106
Donnelly, Kitty, 97
Donnelly, Michael, 110
Dorr, Mrs. Rheta Childe, 75
Dreier, Mary, 116
Dressler, Marie, 94
Duchene, Madame Gabrielle, 212

E

Early inventions, 38
  first power loom, 38
Emerson, Mary, 46
Equal rights by Federal Amendment and state blanket legislation, 164

F

Factory girls, Association, 42
Family wage, 156, 158
Feldman, Bernard, 75
Female Improvement Society, the, 41
Fire hazard, 126
Fire prevention, 127
First factory workers, American born, 39
Fitzgerald, Anna, 95
Fitzpatrick, John, 87
Fredericks, Lillian, 97
Frincke, Augusta J., 98
Funk, Bertha, 121

G

Gillespie, Mabel, 89
Gilman, Charlotte Perkins, 161
Goggin, Catherine, 86
Goldmark, Josephine, 130, 148
Gompers, Samuel, 94, 102, 109
Goodman, Sadie, 84

H

Haig, Ethel, 101
Halas, Mary V., 103
Haley, Margaret, 86
Hamilton, Dr. Alice, 124, 188
Hammond, Professor M. H., 145
Harding, President Warren G., 227
Hart Schaffner & Marx, 83
Hart Schaffner & Marx agreement, 119
Hazardous occupations, 216
Henrotin, Mrs. Charles, 107
Hewes, Amy, 188
Home work, 182
Houck, Daisy, 97

I

Immigrant workers, 48, 79
Immigration, 216
Industrial hygiene, 123
　dangerous trades, 124
　munition factories, 187
　munitions risks, 125, 126
Industrial legislation, 123-142
　advantage of shorter hours, 138
　and the war, 190
　and women, 139
　for men and women, 159
　for women, 129, 135
　helps to standardize industry, 142
　lowering of standards, 188
　opposition to, 137
　Ritchie decision, 147
　standardizing industry, 134
　state laws, 130, 179
　state laws, table of, 132
Infant death rate and wages, 169
International Congress of working women, 214
　first congress, 114
International Federation of Trade Unions, 224
International Federation of working women, 212-228
　agricultural workers, 226
　anthrax, 225
　disarmament, 227
　first international congress, 114
　headquarters in America, 228
　international standards, 215
　program, 223
　program of Polish women, 217
　unemployment, 226
International Labor Conference, 214, 219, 228
Investigations,
　Federal, 1907-11, 168
　Great Britain, 146
　in Australia, 157
　infant death rate, 169
　into the condition of woman and child wage earners, 160
　munitions risks, 188
　Negro women in industry, 203
　New York State Factory Commission, 127
　Niagara Falls, 175
　regulation of labor, 51
　Victoria, 143

INDEX

J

Johnson, Agnes, 98
Joint Board of Sanitary Control, 82

K

Katzor, Clara, 97
Kelleher, Mary 95
Kelley, Florence, 147
Kenney, Mary (Mrs. Mary Kenney O'Sullivan), 54, 107
Knights of Labor, 51, 107
Konopska, Felice, 215

L

Lamphere, Emma, 97
Lemlich, Clara, 79
Leon, Clara, 83
Lewis, Augusta, 96
Limitation of hours, 214
 first asked, 45-47
 for men, 141
 1847, 129
 1852, 129
 1876-9, 1898, 129-130
 Illinois, 1915, 130
Lindstrom, Ellen, 97
Linehan, Peter F., 89
Loeb Rule, 86
Long, Nora, 98
Lowell Factory Girls' Association, 42
Lowell, Josephine Shaw, 55
Lowell Labor Reform Association, 45

M

Macarthur, Mary, 146
Majerova, Madame, 215
Maloney, Elizabeth, 97
Manicom, Kate, 227
Married women, 160
Maternity insurance, 156, 214, 216
McDowell, Mary E., 167

McEnerney, Mary, 97
Meehan, Mary E., 98
Metz, Edith Souter, 97
Minimum wage, 143-165
 and Women's Trade Union League, 146
 bill in Great Britain in 1795, 143
 Canada, 154
 decrees, 131
 in Great Britain, 146
 in New Zealand, 145
 in Victoria, 143
 Massachusetts, 148, 153
 Nebraska, 153
 Oregon case, 149
 rates, 150
 Texas, 153
 wage board procedure, 145
Mitchell, Louisa M., 41
Moran, Mary E., 98
Morgan, Thomas G., 53
Morgan, Mrs. Thomas G., 54
Morris, Max, 110
Mother's pensions, 131, 156
Mullaney, Kate, 74

N

Nason, Mary A., 97
National Consumers League, 56, 130
National Industrial Congress, 44
National Woman's Party, 163
National Young Women's Christian Association, 193
Neary, Anna, 95, 98
Negro men and women in trade unions, 210
Negro slavery, 46
Negro women, 121, 177, 202-211
 and factory conditions, 205
 and race relations, 207
 and seasonal trades, 206
 and the department stores, 205
 and wages, 205
 in Chicago, 208
 in Decatur, Illinois, 209
 in Detroit, 209
 in metal trades, 204
 in needle trades, 204

Negro women,
  in Newark, New Jersey, 209
  investigation of, in industry, 203
  report of Women's Bureau, 202
Negro workers, 102
Nestor, Agnes, 97
Night work, 216

O

Obenauer, Marie, 170
O'Brien, John, 110
O'Connor, Julia, 97
Occupational statistics, 161
Occupations,
  automobile industry, 209
  baking and candy making, 59
  boot and shoe workers, 60
  bottling, 60
  bookbinding, 59
  biologists, 92
  car cleaners, 62
  clerks, 92
  cigar making, 63
  cap makers, 117
  corset workers, 119
  car conductors, 198
  doctors, 92
  department store employees, 205
  domestic, 209
  electrical workers, 64
  editors, 92
  foundry work, 210
  flagmaking, 92
  furriers, 64
  glass blowing, 61
  glove making, 66
  government employment, 90
  hat making, 61
  janitresses, 209
  investigators, 92
  librarians, 92
  leather work, 69
  laundry work, 68
  matrons, 92
  metal trades, 195, 204
  mining, 210
  Negro women, 202–211

Occupations,
  needle trades, 72, 76, 204, 209
  nurses, 92
  office work, 208, 209
  of women, statistics, 57
  postoffice clerk, 69
  printing, 70
  packing trades, 69, 206
  railway clerks, 63
  restaurant work, 67
  railroad telegraphers, 70
  shoe making, 40, 55, 77
  shirt and collar industry, 73
  statisticians, 92
  stenographers, 92
  stage performers, 93
  steel industry, 206
  textiles, 194
  timber working, 196
  telephone operating, 88
  teaching, 86
  typists, 92
  textile industry, 37, 72, 76
  tobacco making, 40
  upholstering, 70
Official appointment trade union women, 192
Ordnance Department, 173
O'Reilly, Leonora, 55
O'Reilly, Mary, 51
O'Sullivan, John F., 108
O'Sullivan, Mary Kenney, 54, 109
Overwork, 180, 181
Owen, Robert Dale, 43

P

Paterson, Emma, 109
Poland, 215
Post, Louis F., 166
Poyntz, Juliet Stuart, 82
Primitive woman in industry, 23-30
  as a producer, 25
  as agriculturist, 26, 28
  as inventor and creator, 25
  her achievements, 24
  her social power, 29
Protocol, the, 80

INDEX 239

R

Rankin, Jeannette, 191
Rankin, Mildred, 121
Ritchie case, 1893, 130
Robins, Mrs. Raymond, 115, 219
Rodgers, Mrs. George, 107
Rosa, Dr. E. B., quoted, 92
Russell Sage Foundation, 173

S

Sanitation a century ago, 39
Santora, Mamie, 98
Schneiderman, Rose, 117, 121, 213
Scott, Melinda, 95
Seasonal trades, 140, 206
Shepherd, Miriam, 219
Shields, Emma L., 203
Shoe makers, 47
Short hours approved by employers, 189
Smith, Charlotte, 52
Snyder, Anna, 83
Source list of references and reading, 232
Standards in industry, 192
State women's bureaus, 185
Steghageu, Emma, 97, 107
Stevens, Alzina P., 107
Stokes, Miss, 75
Stone, Huldah, 46
"Strike of the Forty Thousand," 117
Strikes, 67, 79, 80, 117
  Boston policemen's strike, 118
  children's, 116
  first strike, 41
  Troy laundry workers', 1869 and 1905, 74
Stychova, Madame, 215
Swartz, Mrs. Maud, 121, 219

T

Tansey, James, 110
Ten-hour day, 45
Terry, Mary, 75
Thompson, Mary, 121
Tobin, John P., 110
Townsend, Fannie Lee, 46

Trade unions, national and local,
  Actors' Equity Association, 93
  Amalgamated Clothing Workers of America, 71, 78, 83
  Amalgamated Meat Cutters and Butcher Workmen of North America, 69, 110
  Amalgamated Sheet Metal Workers' International Alliance, 100
  American Federation of Labor, 51, 93, 96, 101, 108
  American Federation of Teachers, 87
  American Federation of Textile Operatives, 72
  Bakery and Confectionery Workers, 59
  Boot and Shoe Workers Union, 54, 60, 77, 78
  Boston Central Labor Body, 43
  Chorus girls, 94
  Cigar Makers International Union, 53, 63
  Daughters of St. Crispin, 47
  Federal Labor Union, Women's, 107
  Federation of Labor, Chicago, 82, 86
  Female Labor Reform Association, 45
  first women's, 40
  foreign unions, 221
  fur workers, 78
  glass bottle blowers, 61
  glove workers, 78
  hotel and restaurant employees, 54, 67
  Industrial Congress at Boston, 46
  International Association of Machinists, 100
  International Brotherhood of Electrical Workers, 64
  International Brotherhood of Bookbinders, 59
  International Brotherhood of Foundry Employees, 100
  International Fur Workers Union, 64

240 WOMEN AND THE LABOR MOVEMENT

Trade unions, national and local,
  International Glove Workers of America, 66
  International Ladies Garment Workers, 53, 78, 110
  International Metal Polishers' Union, 100
  International Molders' Union, 99, 100
  International Typographical Union, The, 70
  International Union of Timber Workers, 101
  International Union of United Brewery, Flour, Cereal and Soft Drinks Workers, 60
  Journeyman Barbers' International Union, 99
  Knights of Labor, 50
  Knights of St. Crispin, 47
  Industrial Workers of the World, 73
  International Ladies Garment Workers, 65
  International Workingmen's Association, 49
  Labor Reform Associations, 46
  Lowell Female Labor Reform Association, 45
  Laundry Workers International Union, 68
  National Federation of Federal Employes, 90
  National Federation of Postoffice Clerks, 69
  National Trade Union, 42
  new developments, 230
  New England Labor Reform League, 46
  New England Working Men's Association, 44, 45
  Parasol and Umbrella Makers' Union, 109
  Railway Carmen, 62
  Railway and Steamship Clerks, 63
  railroad telegraphers, 70
  retail clerks, 110
  Retail Clerks' International Protective Union, 110
  reefer makers, 79

Trade unions, national and local,
  Shirt Sewers' Union, 44
  shoe binders, 43
  shoe workers, 110
  teachers, 86
  telephone operators, 88
  Telephone Operators Department, 90
  textile workers, 110
  "The Female Society of Lynn and Vicinity," 43
  Troy Federation of Labor, 75
  Typographical Union, 53
  United Brotherhood of Carpenters and Joiners, 99, 101
  United Cloth Hat and Cap Makers, 61, 78
  United Garment Workers of America, 54, 65, 78, 82, 110
  United Hatters, 78
  United Leather Workers, 69
  United States Shoe Workers of America, 73
  United Textile Workers, 53, 72
  Upholsterers' International Union, 70, 95
  White Goods Workers of Paris, 228
  Working Women's Association of New York, 48
  Woman's National Industrial League, 52
  Working Women's Protective Union, 48, 109
  Working Women's Society of New York, 55
  Women's Typographical Union, 109
  Women's Union in the Bureau of Engraving and Printing, 90
Triangle Fire, 118
Tulloch, Ethel E., 98

U

Unemployment, 216
United States Ordnance Department, 114

INDEX   241

V

Valesh, Eva McDonald, 54
Van Etten, Ida, 54
Van Kleeck, Mary, 173, 177

W

Wages, 42
Waight, Lavinia, 41
Walling, William English, 109
War Labor Administration, 191
Wilson, William B., 114, 166, 191
Wilson, President Woodrow, 114
White, Harry, 110
Woman in Industry Service, 175, 176
Woman Suffrage, 44, 48, 49
Women and admission to unions, 98
  and economic struggles, 104
  and machine industry in England in eighteenth century, 37
  and new opportunities, 201
  and positions of leadership, 98, 112, 113
  as car conductors, 198
  as organizers, 96, 111, 112
  as technical advisers, 215
Women in Industry Committee of the Council of National Defense, 114
Women in the home, 162
Women in War-Time Industries, 186-201
  lumber, 196
Women in War-Time Industries, metals, 195
  textiles, 194
Women's auxiliaries, 104
Women's Bureau, 166-185, reports, 178
Women's Division, 168, 169
Women's International League for Peace and Freedom, 227
Women's Trade Union League, National and Local, 75, 80, 89, 95, 102, 106-122, 166, 213, 214, 228
  and fire prevention, 118
  and legislation, 111, 120
  and minimum wage, 146
  and organization, 111, 118, 119
  and the Women's Bureau, 113
  and vocational training, 114
  Boston, 118
  British, 109
  Chicago, 119
  Federal Labor Union, Women's, 108
  its philosophy, 122
  Kansas City Convention, 114
  national convention, 98
  New York, 116
  program, 113
Woodhull, Victoria, 49
Workers Education, 81, 84
  Bryn Mawr Summer School, 120
  Training School for Women Organizers, 120
Working Men's Party, 44
Wright, Frances, 43

EDITORIAL COMMITTEE

The Workers' Bookshelf

CHARLES A. BEARD

JOHN R. COMMONS

FANNIA M. COHN

H. W. L. DANA

JOHN P. FREY

ARTHUR GLEASON

WALTON HAMILTON

EVERETT DEAN MARTIN

SPENCER MILLER, JR.

GEORGE W. PERKINS

FLORENCE C. THORNE

MATTHEW WOLL

ROBERT B. WOLF

American Labor: From Conspiracy to Collective Bargaining

AN ARNO PRESS/NEW YORK TIMES COLLECTION

SERIES I

Abbott, Edith.
Women in Industry. 1913.

Aveling, Edward B. and Eleanor M. Aveling.
Working Class Movement in America. 1891.

Beard, Mary.
The American Labor Movement. 1939.

Blankenhorn, Heber.
The Strike for Union. 1924.

Blum, Solomon.
Labor Economics. 1925.

Brandeis, Louis D. and Josephine Goldmark.
Women in Industry. 1907. New introduction by Leon Stein and Philip Taft.

Brooks, John Graham.
American Syndicalism. 1913.

Butler, Elizabeth Beardsley.
Women and the Trades. 1909.

Byington, Margaret Frances.
Homestead: The Household of A Mill Town. 1910.

Carroll, Mollie Ray.
Labor and Politics. 1923.

Coleman, McAlister.
Men and Coal. 1943.

Coleman, J. Walter.
The Molly Maguire Riots: Industrial Conflict in the Pennsylvania Coal Region. 1936.

Commons, John R.
Industrial Goodwill. 1919.

Commons, John R.
Industrial Government. 1921.

Dacus, Joseph A.
Annals of the Great Strikes. 1877.

Dealtry, William.
The Laborer: A Remedy for his Wrongs. 1869.

Douglas, Paul H., Curtis N. Hitchcock and Willard E. Atkins, editors.
The Worker in Modern Economic Society. 1923.

Eastman, Crystal.
Work Accidents and the Law. 1910.

Ely, Richard T.
The Labor Movement in America. 1890. New Introduction by Leon Stein and Philip Taft.

Feldman, Herman.
Problems in Labor Relations. 1937.

Fitch, John Andrew.
The Steel Worker. 1910.

Furniss, Edgar S. and Laurence Guild.
Labor Problems. 1925.

Gladden, Washington.
Working People and Their Employers. 1885.

Gompers, Samuel.
Labor and the Common Welfare. 1919.

Hardman, J. B. S., editor.
American Labor Dynamics. 1928.

Higgins, George G.
Voluntarism in Organized Labor, 1930-40. 1944.

Hiller, Ernest T.
The Strike. 1928.

Hollander, Jacob S. and George E. Barnett.
Studies in American Trade Unionism. 1906. New Introduction by Leon Stein and Philip Taft.

Jelley, Symmes M.
The Voice of Labor. 1888.

Jones, Mary.
Autobiography of Mother Jones. 1925.

Kelley, Florence.
Some Ethical Gains Through Legislation. 1905.

LaFollette, Robert M., editor.
The Making of America: Labor. 1906.

Lane, Winthrop D.
Civil War in West Virginia. 1921.

Lauck, W. Jett and Edgar Sydenstricker.
Conditions of Labor in American Industries. 1917.

Leiserson, William M.
Adjusting Immigrant and Industry. 1924.

Lescohier, Don D.
Knights of St. Crispin. 1910.

Levinson, Edward.
I Break Strikes. The Technique of Pearl L. Bergoff. 1935.

Lloyd, Henry Demarest.
Men, The Workers. Compiled by Anne Whithington and Caroline Stallbohen. 1909. New Introduction by Leon Stein and Philip Taft.

Lorwin, Louis (Louis Levine).
The Women's Garment Workers. 1924.

Markham, Edwin, Ben B. Lindsay and George Creel.
Children in Bondage. 1914.

Marot, Helen.
American Labor Unions. 1914.

Mason, Alpheus T.
Organized Labor and the Law. 1925.

Newcomb, Simon.
A Plain Man's Talk on the Labor Question. 1886. New Introduction by Leon Stein and Philip Taft.

Price, George Moses.
The Modern Factory: Safety, Sanitation and Welfare. 1914.

Randall, John Herman Jr.
Problem of Group Responsibility to Society. 1922.

Rubinow, I. M.
Social Insurance. 1913.

Saposs, David, editor.
Readings in Trade Unionism. 1926.

Slichter, Sumner H.
Union Policies and Industrial Management. 1941.

Socialist Publishing Society.
The Accused and the Accusers. 1887.

Stein, Leon and Philip Taft, editors.
The Pullman Strike. 1894-1913. New Introduction by the editors.

Stein, Leon and Philip Taft, editors.
Religion, Reform, and Revolution: Labor Panaceas in the Nineteenth Century. 1969. New Introduction by the editors.

Stein, Leon and Philip Taft, editors.
Wages, Hours, and Strikes: Labor Panaceas in the Twentieth Century. 1969. New introduction by the editors.

Swinton, John.
A Momentous Question: The Respective Attitudes of Labor and Capital. 1895. New Introduction by Leon Stein and Philip Taft.

Tannenbaum, Frank.
The Labor Movement. 1921.

Tead, Ordway.
Instincts in Industry. 1918.

Vorse, Mary Heaton.
Labor's New Millions. 1938.

Witte, Edwin Emil.
The Government in Labor Disputes. 1932.

Wright, Carroll D.
The Working Girls of Boston. 1889.

Wyckoff, Veitrees J.
Wage Policies of Labor Organizations in a Period of Industrial Depression. 1926.

Yellen, Samuel.
American Labor Struggles. 1936.

SERIES II

Allen, Henry J.
The Party of the Third Part: The Story of the Kansas Industrial Relations Court. 1921. *Including* **The Kansas Court of Industrial Relations Law** (1920) by Samuel Gompers.

Baker, Ray Stannard.
The New Industrial Unrest. 1920.

Barnett, George E. & David A. McCabe.
Mediation, Investigation and Arbitration in Industrial Disputes. 1916.

Barns, William E., editor.
The Labor Problem. 1886.

Bing, Alexander M.
War-Time Strikes and Their Adjustment. 1921.

Brooks, Robert R. R.
When Labor Organizes. 1937.

Calkins, Clinch.
Spy Overhead: The Story of Industrial Espionage. 1937.

Cooke, Morris Llewellyn & Philip Murray.
Organized Labor and Production. 1940.

Creamer, Daniel & Charles W. Coulter.
Labor and the Shut-Down of the Amoskeag Textile Mills. 1939.

Glocker, Theodore W.
The Government of American Trade Unions. 1913.

Gompers, Samuel.
Labor and the Employer. 1920.

Grant, Luke.
The National Erectors' Association and the International Association of Bridge and Structural Ironworkers. 1915.

Haber, William.
Industrial Relations in the Building Industry. 1930.

Henry, Alice.
Women and the Labor Movement. 1923.

Herbst, Alma.
The Negro in the Slaughtering and Meat-Packing Industry in Chicago. 1932.

[Hicks, Obediah.]
Life of Richard F. Trevellick. 1896.

Hillquit, Morris, Samuel Gompers & Max J. Hayes.
The Double Edge of Labor's Sword: Discussion and Testimony on Socialism and Trade-Unionism Before the Commission on Industrial Relations. 1914. New Introduction by Leon Stein and Philip Taft.

Jensen, Vernon H.
Lumber and Labor. 1945.

Kampelman, Max M.
The Communist Party vs. the C.I.O. 1957.

Kingsbury, Susan M., editor.
Labor Laws and Their Enforcement. By Charles E. Persons, Mabel Parton, Mabelle Moses & Three "Fellows." 1911.

McCabe, David A.
The Standard Rate in American Trade Unions. 1912.

Mangold, George Benjamin.
Labor Argument in the American Protective Tariff Discussion. 1908.

Millis, Harry A., editor.
How Collective Bargaining Works. 1942.

Montgomery, Royal E.
Industrial Relations in the Chicago Building Trades. 1927.

Oneal, James.
The Workers in American History. 3rd edition, 1912.

Palmer, Gladys L.
Union Tactics and Economic Change: A Case Study of Three Philadelphia Textile Unions. 1932.

Penny, Virginia.
How Women Can Make Money: Married or Single, In all Branches of the Arts and Sciences, Professions, Trades, Agricultural and Mechanical Pursuits. 1870. New Introduction by Leon Stein and Philip Taft.

Penny, Virginia.
Think and Act: A Series of Articles Pertaining to Men and Women, Work and Wages. 1869.

Pickering, John.
The Working Man's Political Economy. 1847.

Ryan, John A.
A Living Wage. 1906.

Savage, Marion Dutton.
Industrial Unionism in America. 1922.

Simkhovitch, Mary Kingsbury.
The City Worker's World in America. 1917.

Spero, Sterling Denhard.
The Labor Movement in a Government Industry: A Study of Employee Organization in the Postal Service. 1927.

Stein, Leon and Philip Taft, editors.
Labor Politics: Collected Pamphlets. 2 vols. 1836-1932. New Introduction by the editors.

Stein, Leon and Philip Taft, editors.
The Management of Workers: Selected Arguments. 1917-1956. New Introduction by the editors.

Stein, Leon and Philip Taft, editors.
Massacre at Ludlow: Four Reports. 1914-1915. New Introduction by the editors.

Stein, Leon and Philip Taft, editors.
Workers Speak: Self-Portraits. 1902-1906. New Introduction by the editors.

Stolberg, Benjamin.
The Story of the CIO. 1938.

Taylor, Paul S.
The Sailors' Union of the Pacific. 1923.

U.S. Commission on Industrial Relations.
Efficiency Systems and Labor. 1916. New Introduction by Leon Stein and Philip Taft.

Walker, Charles Rumford.
American City: A Rank-and-File History. 1937.

Walling, William English.
American Labor and American Democracy. 1926.

Williams, Whiting.
What's on the Worker's Mind: By One Who Put on Overalls to Find Out. 1920.

Wolman, Leo.
The Boycott in American Trade Unions. 1916.

Ziskind, David.
One Thousand Strikes of Government Employees. 1940.